SOMEONE TO LOVE
How to find romance in the personal columns

MARGARET NELSON has worked as a counsellor specializing in relationships and is now a freelance writer. This book grew out of her experiences of working with divorced people who were 'beginning again'. She is a member of the British Association of Counsellors. This is her first book.

Overcoming Common Problems Series

The ABC of Eating
Coping with anorexia, bulimia and
compulsive eating
JOY MELVILLE

An A–Z of Alternative Medicine
BRENT Q. HAFEN AND KATHRYN J.
FRANDSEN

Arthritis
Is your suffering really necessary?
DR WILLIAM FOX

Being the Boss
STEPHEN FITZSIMON

Birth Over Thirty
SHEILA KITZINGER

Body Language
How to read others' thoughts by their gestures
ALLAN PEASE

Calm Down
How to cope with frustration and anger
DR PAUL HAUCK

Comfort for Depression
JANET HORWOOD

Common Childhood Illnesses
DR PATRICIA GILBERT

Complete Public Speaker
GYLES BRANDRETH

Coping with Depression and Elation
DR PATRICK McKEON

Coping Successfully with Your Child's Asthma
DR PAUL CARSON

**Coping Successfully with Your Child's Skin
Problems**
DR PAUL CARSON

**Coping Successfully with Your Hyperactive
Child**
DR PAUL CARSON

Curing Arthritis Cookbook
MARGARET HILLS

Curing Arthritis – The Drug-free Way
MARGARET HILLS

Curing Illness – The Drug-free Way
MARGARET HILLS

Depression
DR PAUL HAUCK

Divorce and Separation
ANGELA WILLANS

The Epilepsy Handbook
SHELAGH McGOVERN

Everything You Need to Know about Adoption
MAGGIE JONES

**Everything You Need to Know about Contact
Lenses**
DR ROBERT YOUNGSON

**Everything You Need to Know about the
Pill**
WENDY COOPER AND TOM SMITH

Everything You Need to Know about Shingles
DR ROBERT YOUNGSON

Family First Aid and Emergency Handbook
DR ANDREW STANWAY

Feverfew
A traditional herbal remedy for migraine and
arthritis
DR STEWART JOHNSON

Fight Your Phobia and Win
DAVID LEWIS

Flying Without Fear
TESSA DUCKWORTH AND DAVID
MILLER

Goodbye Backache
DR DAVID IMRIE WITH COLLEEN
DIMSON

Overcoming Common Problems Series

Overcoming Common Problems Series

Overcoming Common Problems

SOMEONE TO LOVE

Margaret Nelson

SHELDON PRESS
LONDON

First published in Great Britain in 1988 by
Sheldon Press, SPCK, Marylebone Road, London NW1 4DU

We are grateful to *Private Eye* magazine
for permission to reproduce the story on page 83.

All the examples given in the book are fictional,
and no reference is intended to any real person.

British Library Cataloguing in Publication Data
Nelson, Margaret
    Someone to love: how to find romance in
    the personal columns. —— (Overcoming
    common problems).
    1. Newspapers with British imprints.
    Personal columns
    I. Title   II. Series
    070.4'42

    ISBN 0–85969–574–3

Typeset by Deltatype Ltd, Ellesmere Port, Cheshire
Printed in Great Britain by Richard Clay Ltd, Bungay, Suffolk

To Pat and Chris Oliver, with thanks.

Contents

Introduction

There are 9 000 000 single people of marriageable age living in Britain today. Many of them are lonely, and because of their job, their shyness, their geographical location or the responsibility of children from a failed marriage, they are unable to find the type of social life which enables them to widen their circle of friends, or to find someone with whom they can settle down.

Pubs, discos, clubs and classes are not to everyone's liking, and most activities, limited as they are to comparatively small groups of people, do not present the individual with the opportunity to meet large numbers of people.

Marriage bureaux have their successes, but they can be expensive and with the growing army of divorced people seeking a second chance, there have been reports of 'cowboy'-type operations. Matchmakers setting up a new business in this industry are sometimes most reticent about revealing how many prospects they have on their books.

Using classified advertising in trying to broaden one's social life and to find a permanent partner is not new. In Britain it began in the eighteenth century when a gentleman's eye may have been caught by an attractive lady at the theatre or opera. The next morning *her* eye might be caught by a line or two in the daily London press – referring to her whereabouts the previous night, perhaps to the colour of her dress and fan – and asking her to make contact, with a box number. . . .

In postwar years, this type of advertising was seen as the medium for people who were unable to meet partners in a 'normal' way because of lack of social skills, poor education or simply poverty.

This is no longer the case. A look at statistics gathered by the largest organization (Singles Scene Ltd, 8th July 1987) specializing in providing a medium for personal classified advertising shows that 45 per cent of male advertisers and 40 per cent of female advertisers have been educated to 'A' level or above. This includes 21 per cent of men, and 17 per cent of women with degrees; 63 per cent of all advertisers own their own homes.

As the heartsearch column becomes more respectable, it gains in popularity, and is seen by many as a growing necessity in modern life – particularly for the thousands who suffer the anonymity which city-dwelling inevitably brings.

By judicious use of the heartsearch columns the fugitive from loneliness can be presented with, at small cost, a large number of prospects for a relationship. The advertiser can retain complete control of whom he or she meets, secure in the knowledge that there are plenty of appropriate people 'out there'. With patience and common sense the advertiser will eventually meet the person for whom he or she is looking.

But the heartsearch column has both an inner and an outer danger. The danger from outside is presented by the person who is not looking for, and indeed may not be capable of, a normal sharing relationship. The inner danger is the ease with which seekers project the image of their 'ideal partner' onto a person who is nothing of the kind.

This book aims to help the reader to make the most of the heartsearch columns, to avoid the outer dangers, and to recognize the difference between inner ideals – and reality.

NB A useful address for readers of this book is: The Association of British Introduction Agencies, 29 Manchester Street, London, W1. Telephone: 01–938 1011

1

Advertising Can Work

> Attractive divorcee, 43, warm and caring, seeks lasting
> relationship, perhaps marriage, with solvent professional
> man, 45–55. Enjoys music, cinema, walking, pets, cook-
> ing. North. Photo appreciated. Box 777.

Sounds simple enough, doesn't it? There must be thousands of
single men who would jump at the chance of meeting the lady
who advertises as above. Perhaps she will be deluged with
willing suitors, swept away by knights in shining armour,
wined and dined, wedded and bedded. Perhaps somewhere
out there waits the one man who shares her interests, will fulfil
her dreams, and to whom she can give all the warmth and
caring which, at the moment, has no focus. Perhaps they will
exchange a few letters, one or two telephone calls, meet, fall
in love and live happily ever after.

But – is it as simple as that? Is the swiftly growing singles
'industry' really working for its users? Is it so easy to find a
loving and lasting relationship by spending a few pounds on an
advertisement, or should the heartsearch columns be more
appropriately called heartache columns?

There are many hidden dangers in this world of emotional
meetings with complete strangers, but the experience of
many people suggests that with thought and a large helping of
luck, it *is* possible to meet the 'right' person through these
columns.

Lonely, but not alone

When you return to your house each evening and sit,
wondering whether you will ever have a partner to come home

to, of course you feel lonely – but you are certainly not alone. A quick look at the figures below will tell you how many others are in the same or a similar position.

During 1985, there were 160000 divorces granted in England and Wales. This means that 320000 men and women, who had thought at one time that they were settled with a partner for life, were back on the marriage market. The table below shows how this figure breaks down into age groups, and you can see that although the peak is in the late twenties and early thirties, there are still significant numbers right up to sixty-year-olds. These figures do not include the many who have lost a spouse through death, but because of their established pattern of life no longer have the habit of 'going out to meet people'.

Divorce figures for the year 1985 – England and Wales; total number of divorced persons: 320 574

Ages of parties	
up to 29 years	106 929
up to 39 years	115 233
up to 49 years	64 090
up to 59 years	24 655
over 60 years	9667

There are many reasons for the enormous number of marital breakdowns, and many books have been written on the subject, but if *you* are one of those divorce statistics, the first thing you must have is a belief that most human beings, yourself included, have the ability to learn from their mistakes.

Many older people can feel very despairing about finding a partner, thinking that the older they get the less likely they are to find someone of a suitable age. This is not true – one of the reasons that there are fewer available *divorced* persons in the sixty-plus group is because they are more likely to have lost a partner through death, rather than divorce.

Things are different now

Perhaps you ask yourself why you are finding it so difficult to meet another partner, or why your social life seems non-existent, and wonder if there is something wrong with you.

Do not blame yourself. In our modern world it is harder for people to meet suitable partners. Hundreds of years ago there was not the same differentiation between people. Individuals did not move home so frequently. They grew up and lived in small communities, where most interests were shared and understood by all. Expectations of life were the same for most people, and the need to work together for survival made it imperative for people to 'get on' together. A modern husband and wife can, and often do, spend hours arguing about the most trivial things, and the marriage counsellors will be standing by with myriad explanations. The medieval farmer and his wife would quickly find, if they spent as much time as we do in talking and arguing, that the cows had wandered over into the wrong pasture, or the grain, so necessary for next winter's survival, had been lost.

But the changing face of our society has not changed the basic need of each one of us to have our own 'special' person, with whom to enjoy all the good things of life; someone to share things with when we are happy, and when we are sad; someone with whom we can express our sexuality; someone whom we can trust through thick and thin to be there when we need them and to whom we can offer the same comfort that they offer us.

Most men and women who turn to the heartsearch columns to find a partner will have two things in common in addition to their wish to find that special someone. They will probably have exhausted the direct methods of meeting people – at work, clubs and classes, and their own circle of friends, most of whom may be married or in a relationship; and they may feel rejected and 'bad' because of the failure of their previous relationships. Hopefully they will have looked carefully at their own contribution to these failures and learned something of their own weaknesses, both in choice and behaviour, and will be determined to make a new start, using the insights they have gained.

But this is not always the case – there are many who, because of repeated failures, have become cynical, and these are the people who have no intention of making a permanent commitment to anyone. These people are not always easy to recognize, and they may not even recognize their own intentions, but sadly they are the ones who see people as new experiences to be thrown aside as they go in search of the next adventure. Chapter 10 attempts to give you the means to recognize these people early enough in a new relationship to avoid being hurt by them.

What you will find in this book is based on the real experiences of many men and women who have used advertising to seek a deep and lasting relationship. Some of them found what they needed, some did not. By following the fairly detailed suggestions, you will see how to avoid wasting the time and emotional energy that is needed in your search.

There is, of course, no guarantee that you will find the man or woman of your dreams, but you will approach the task feeling more confident that you can read the signs. Because the search will be less anxious, it will be more exciting and certainly give you insights into your own, and others', behaviour.

You can most definitely have a lot of fun using the heartsearch columns, and – who knows – perhaps you will find the new start you are looking for; the relationship that may last a lifetime.

2

How to Start

The publications

Many magazines available in Britain include some heart-search advertisements. Most local newspapers carry a few in their 'Personal' columns – *The London and Local Advertiser*, for example, publishes some 200 heartsearch advertisements every week. But some publications appearing nationally are quite well-known for the large numbers of replies they forward each month to their advertisers. This chapter tells you what you need to know about them and what sort of response you can expect.

Singles Magazine

The only widely circulated magazine entirely devoted to the heartsearch industry is *Singles Magazine*. It is published monthly in London and carries about 1000 advertisements in each issue, clearly divided into 'male' and 'female' sections. In the more recent issues, 'men looking for women' outnumber 'women looking for men' by about two to one. The youngest advertisers are eighteen years old, the oldest are in their seventies. So you are never either too old or too young to start.

Singles regards itself as the advertising medium for the 'ordinary' men and women who are seeking a heterosexual relationship which may lead to marriage. It does not attract the type of person who would generally be regarded as 'kinky', and is careful to maintain a standard which would not offend any of its readers. It includes articles, readers' letters and an advice column specifically for people who are having trouble finding a relationship.

Singles costs £1, and claims a circulation of 23 000 per month. Over 17 000 replies per month are forwarded to advertisers – that is an average of seventeen replies per advertisement. At the time of writing, an average-sized advertisement will cost about £20, and as much as £50 with the addition of a photograph and extra wording. If you are careful in your choice of words, you should be able to get good value for your money for very little more than the basic rate of £15.

The record number of responses to an advertisement in *Singles* is 250. These were to a 'Well-travelled graduate', and his advertisement included a very good photograph and about sixty words – bringing its cost to over £70.

With very few exceptions, box numbers are used by advertisers, so that all replies go to the magazine. The reason for this is fairly obvious – if you put your address, or even your telephone number on a heartsearch advertisement, you risk unwelcome visitors or calls. People replying to advertisements are asked to post all their replies – each in its own envelope, with the box number and a first-class or second-class stamp on it – to the address of the magazine. The individual envelopes are then readdressed to the advertisers, and posted separately. Within days of *Singles* appearing on the bookstalls, you can expect replies. Your box number will remain active for twelve months, though most of your post will arrive during the first two weeks after publication.

New Statesman

Two other nationally circulated magazines are worth noting. The first is *New Statesman* which has a small section of heartsearch advertisements in its classified columns: the current issue shows twenty-five advertisements, roughly half men and half women. While this is not a great number of advertisers, they tend – because of the nature of the magazine – to be rather intellectual and generally left-wing. *New Statesman* does not run the more kinky, and even openly perverted advertisements that can be seen in other places, though they will accept an advertisement from a person who states quite openly that he or she is married, and looking for a little amusement on the side.

The advertising rates are very reasonable, and you can buy enough words in *New Statesman* to describe yourself adequately for about half the price of a *Singles* ad. *New Statesman's* circulation is 30000 per week, and it claims that the average number of replies to a heartsearch advertisement is fifteen; the record number, in reply to a young woman, is seventy-one. But she didn't find her dream man, and was back with another advertisement the following week!

Private Eye

Private Eye has a section called 'Eyelove'. *Private Eye*, with a circulation of 230000, claims a readership of 1.3 million. They describe their readers as 'varied and discerning', and are very careful, despite the broadminded nature of the magazine, not to let in any advertisement which might lead to 'humiliation' – that is people looking for partners for abnormal sexual activities. *Private Eye* claim an average of thirty replies to an advertisement in the first week, ten the next, tailing off to six or seven in the third week. The record number of replies to one advertisement was a total of 300 – to a lady who mentioned that she 'enjoyed talking in bed'!

Other publications

There are other publications, such as *Time Out* and *Loot*, in which you can place or answer an advertisement, but they are not editorially as discerning as the three mentioned above, and it is not unusual to find a proportion of people who are seeking anything but a lasting relationship, or marriage. Also, unlike *Singles*, both these publications print advertisements for homosexuals seeking partners. You may decide to buy your own copies of some or all of these publications, and get the feel of them before deciding which one to use. Watch out for certain 'code' words. For example, the use of the phrase 'seeks superior woman' has been used by men who are looking for a sadomasochistic relationship. 'Seeks lashings of fun' is a more obvious statement of intent, but even casual use of words like 'uninhibited' should be considered carefully, if you want to avoid ambiguity.

Some journals also have advertisements which have led to romance, although at first sight they may not appear to be heartsearch advertisements at all. Notably, *The Lady*, published monthly with a circulation of 80 000 per month, carries hundreds of advertisements from people looking for nannies or housekeepers. It is no secret that while most of the advertisers are genuinely seeking an employee (rather than a partner), often men in search of 'housekeepers' will proclaim their single status in their advertisement, and this may attract a woman who would like to kill two birds with one stone. . . .

Starting your plan

Making the decision on whether you will place an advertisement yourself, or confine yourself to answering other people's is quite important. Without thought, it is easy to imagine that by answering advertisements rather than placing them you are reaping the benefits of another's effort and money. But this is not so. As we will see, advertisements do not always say what they mean and it is possible to waste hours in replying carefully and at length to perhaps dozens of advertisements, only to find that the people who lie behind them are not as you had imagined them to be.

If *you* are the person placing the advertisement you are immediately at an advantage. You are putting yourself in the position of the chooser, rather than the supplicator; and this is a good psychological position to be in. You know that you will get *some* answers (and this is by no means guaranteed when you reply to another person's advertisement) and the more thought you put into your advertisement, the more you can expect. Then, by careful use of words, you can exclude many who would otherwise reply hopefully – but in fact be hopelessly inappropriate.

Of course there is nothing wrong in replying to advertisements yourself, and it may provide you with an opportunity to begin expressing yourself in letters to people you have never met. It will also give you a time-filler until your advertisement is published, and you begin to receive your own replies. Do remember to put your address (and telephone number, if you wish) in your replies to advertisements. It is surprising how many people forget to do this and so frustrating for the recipient, who may want to reply to you, but has no way of knowing where to contact you. It is also worth while printing your full name below your signature – which may be clear to you, but just an indecipherable scrawl to someone who is not familiar with your handwriting.

The following examples of advertisements will give you an idea of what appears where.

From *Singles*

Successful professional lady, but so lonely
Attractive, intelligent and energetic. Semi-retired and solvent. Seeking special something with man who appreciates loyalty, love and understanding. Likes music, reading, writing, walking, gardening.

Janice, 26
Where have all the men gone? I just want someone to love me. Anyone out there who wants to enjoy eating out, dancing, and home life when there's time. Please send photo. No husbands please. Up to 45 years. I am single, solvent and sociable. Wirral.

11

Journalist/artist

Academic with new career and lifestyle. Outwardly confident, inwardly shy. Interested in museums, tai-chi, talking, pubs with log fires, but not too much alcohol, music, walking, holding hands, and closeness. Esteems honesty, openness, warmth, humour. Solvent, though not a millionaire. Not dark and handsome, more grey and interesting. Energetic, tolerant and gentle. Strong but not a toughie. Libido unaffected by life's little disappointments. Seeking warmth, affection, sharing of values and mutually supportive attitude. Photo please. All letters will be acknowledged. Have car, will travel. If you make room for me, I'll make room for you.

Jim, 32

Edinburgh. Car mechanic. Music, pubs, cinema, disco. Seeks lasting relationship with non-obese loving female. Car owner. Non-smoker.

From *New Statesman*

Doctor in South, 40, separated. Passions for Sibelius and sunsets. Seeks female with passions for anything else.

Hold my hand? I'm female, 40-ish, single, contented, looking for someone to trust. He should be gentle, energetic and intelligent.

From *Private Eye*

Muse needed by solvent, loving and overworking media consultant (53). Become appreciated, even spoilt! Photo please.

I'm 50, 5'5", 9st. Divorced. Outgoing, intelligent, love

Beethoven and I smoke. Mad sense of humour, warm and romantic. Seek 6′ professional male to share better things of life.

From *Time Out*

Two attractive girls, early 20s, seek two trendy males, under 30. Photos please.

Handsome, caring male musician, artist, salesman. Share cuddles, attention, etc. with special female.

From *Loot*

Shy and forlorn black male, 24, 6ft and slim. Seeks friendly girl to help me out of my shell. I am a Cancerian. Photo appreciated.

Wanted, a very special gentleman, any race, anywhere, sincere, responsible and marriage-minded by slim female in late 30s to share goods and bads of life. Genuine replies only, please.

Case history: Josie

I had been alone by choice for three years after my marriage broke up. Then I started to feel lonely and realized that I was ready to try again. But it seemed impossible to meet the right kind of people. I tried some singles club meetings, but it wasn't my scene – I used to sit there feeling the odd one out, while everyone else seemed to be enjoying themselves. Then I began to notice personal advertisements in the local paper. I answered a couple, but found that the men who had placed them had so many replies they could afford to take their pick, and I didn't like that feeling. So I decided to put the boot on the other foot and advertise myself. At first I think I must have been getting a bit desperate, and I would have died rather than let my friends at work know what I was doing. But things went so well that eventually I was actually boasting in the office about the number of replies I'd had. A couple of the single girls I work with tried it. I met quite a few men before Bill turned up. I got quite used to the blind date bit – something I'd never have done, even when I was younger.

I suppose most of the men I'd met from my advertisement took me out a couple of times, and we always parted on good terms. At least we always knew what we were looking for, and there didn't seem to be any resentment when we decided to move on. Bill was different from the start – we both knew that this time it was for real, and the biggest problem we've ever had was telling his mum how we met!

3

The Language of Advertisements

If you have never read a heartsearch column before, the first time you look at one will probably be quite an exciting experience, especially if you have reached the point where you feel you are destined to spend the rest of your life alone. Each advertisement you read will produce a picture in your mind of another lonely person, just waiting to meet you.

There is a certain amount of truth in that, but it is also true that many of those people, despite the picture their advertisement conjures up, will not be for you, and the more you learn about the language of the ad, the more discerning you will become in choosing to whom to reply, and the more able you will be to convey an accurate picture of yourself and your hopes and needs, when you place your own advertisement.

Behind the words

Here are some examples of the type of descriptive words that occur over and over in advertisements.

Attractive	Kind	Solvent	Sincere
Sexy	Shy	Practical	Mature
Funloving	Active	Confident	Warm
Pretty	Stable	Easygoing	Slim
Healthy	Considerate	Affectionate	Romantic
Energetic	Genuine	Non-smoker	Short
Humorous	Intelligent	Tall	Thoughtful
Caring	Quiet		

What lovely straightforward words most of these are! But do they really mean anything when they are applied by people to themselves? Even the most easygoing person will become uptight if trapped in the wrong relationship. What does 'intelligent' mean? Able to win quiz shows or get to the top of the career tree? The quietest person can get angry, and the most affectionate person will not be loving and kind unless they have the right person to be loving and kind to.

You have probably had cause to say about another person at some time or another 'They think they're so kind, friendly, smart, etc, *but*. . . .' This is not to suggest that the use of these words is wrong, or worthless, but remember that there are things about yourself and other people that change depending on who you are with or what the circumstances are.

An example of this is something that many people have experienced in quite a dramatic way. Have you ever been involved in an argument with someone – really going at it hammer and tongs – when suddenly the telephone rings. You answer it and hear the voice of someone with whom you get on very well. Without any effort on your part, your manner will change. You are no longer the angry person you were a moment ago, and you are able to carry out a calm and caring conversation with your friend. Then you put the telephone down, turn back to your protagonist, and are immediately transformed into the 'other self', arguing as heatedly as before.

At this time there would be two different people each willing to describe you in completely different terms. Which, if either, is wholly correct in their description?

But we cannot discount the words that are used in advertisements, for they are what the advertisements are made of, and if nothing else they will usually tell us what the advertiser's values are. A man who describes himself as 'gentle' and 'tender' is unlikely to be an emotionally cold person. A woman who describes herself as 'blonde and busty' may quite likely be one whose relationships tend to exist at a superficial level.

But with all the effort in the world we will not always be able to see the person behind the advertisement until we meet them. Louise, who met Bob through an advertisement, was attracted to him because he said that he had a great sense of humour. His letters were full of puns and quips and he even sent little cartoon drawings which amused her, for she was a person who normally laughed very easily.

But when she eventually met him, she found his company very straining. It was some time before she discovered that he suffered very badly from depression – and spent hours before every meeting with her studying his joke books. It appeared that Bob had thought that if he met someone who had a real sense of humour, it would help him to recover from his depression. This is not to say that his advertisement was dishonest, for he did not enjoy his depressed state and wanted to be able to laugh again. His mistake was in thinking that all he required was a person to laugh with him, when his depression had far deeper roots than that.

Many of the descriptive words apply to physical appearance. Most people who have made good relationships through advertisements have remarked that their partner 'did not look at all as I expected', and it is worth giving some thought to this aspect of the search.

Most of us carry around in our heads a blueprint of how we would like our partners to look. This is often an idealized picture of a member of the opposite sex who is goodlooking (and even that means different things to different people), healthy, strong, kind, happy and reasonably well-off. If you stop reading for a moment, close your eyes, and allow yourself to see in your mind's eye *your* ideal, you may recognize how narrow your choice would be in reality if you limited yourself to this physical type. You may also learn that you seek a person who looks very like some other person from your past – perhaps a parent, or someone with whom you had an unsuccesful affair, or a lost spouse.

Or it could be that you have built up an image that is the

opposite to an important person in your past who denied you your emotional needs.

Frank's mother had been an extremely thin woman, and his experience of her was that she was uncomfortable cuddling him when he was very young. His first marriage was to a woman who had a similar build to his mother, and the marriage was unsuccessful. When he began to advertise, he specified that he wanted a 'large, cuddly' partner. Here he was making the mistake of thinking that *all* slim women are emotionally cold, and *all* large women are emotionally warm, and he was very disappointed when he met his large, cuddly partner to find that she couldn't stand dogs, for Frank lived for his two Labradors.

Certain characteristics about which people feel very strongly are mentioned in advertisements over and over again. Frank was an exception to the rule in his demand for a 'large' woman. Many advertisers state that they do not want to meet 'overweight' or 'obese' people. It seems that shorter men find it difficult to find partners; some women have a hang-up about bald heads. Many women find advertisements for 'blonde' or 'busty' females, or too much emphasis on size ('must be slim', 'size 10 or 12 only, please', etc.), a little offensive.

If you believe that 'good' or 'kind' people come in all shapes and sizes, and that having no hair or being slightly overweight is no reason to be condemned, then maybe you will think it worthwhile identifying any prejudices *you* might have, and challenging them. And try taking a look at the things you may not like about your own appearance – should it really be necessary for you to announce them to any possible partner?

Jack had answered Brenda's advertisement. He had a long correspondence with her, then they spoke on the telephone, and he invited her out for a meal. They met outside a restaurant. Brenda was wearing a cloak, rather than a coat and Jack liked the look of her. But when they went into the restaurant, which was a self-service, Brenda had difficulty managing her tray. Jack realized with a shock that she had an artificial hand. He found this almost impossible to cope with, ate his meal hurriedly, and left, making it obvious that he would not be seeing Brenda again. He thought Brenda should have prepared him for her disability.

If you feel particularly strongly about how a person looks, then the most sensible thing to do is to make sure you have seen a *recent* photograph before becoming too involved. If you think appearances are unimportant, you may not wish to make contact with people who ask for photographs – but bear in mind that even if you believe that it *shouldn't* matter what people look like, it is one of the peculiarities of human beings that most of the time it *does* matter, whether we want it to or not.

Liz asked for photographs in her advertisement, but when it came to sending photographs of herself in return, she became annoyed and self-conscious. She discussed this with a friend and realized that she felt very unsure of her own appearance. She was worried that when she actually met someone, they would not like her looks, and she might suffer the embarrassment of being left standing, or rejected within a few minutes of the meeting. Luckily, her friend was supportive and understanding enough to help Liz see that she was no more or less attractive than the majority of women, and she invested in a good photograph, and took the plunge.

Give or take a few years. . . .

It is well worth having a special photograph taken, and getting several prints made, for it is likely that you will need to send them to more than one person. The number of people who use photographs which are slightly out of focus – one suspects to conceal age – is amazingly high! As the intention is usually to meet the person to whom the photograph is sent, it hardly seems worthwhile trying to mislead them; this will inevitably end in disappointment, probably on both sides. The same applies to the use of old photographs. It is sad that many women feel it is to their advantage to use photographs of themselves in swimming costumes, suggesting that their physical features are the most important thing they have to offer. Sadder still when they have to admit that the photograph was taken ten years ago.

On the subject of age – it is a fact that many people have strong ideas about what is a suitable match as far as age difference is concerned. Most people would consider that a man should be older than his partner by anything from one to ten years. Yet many male advertisers state quite unashamedly in their adverts that they are hoping to find a much younger woman. Older women can justifiably be upset by this although there are many younger women who are happy to accept the advances of older men. This may be because they are seeking a 'father-figure', or it may be that they are attracted by a man who already 'has it made' financially. These days it is not such a stigma for an older woman to seek and form a relationship with a much younger man.

What the future of a marriage between an older man and a younger woman might be is open to speculation. Perhaps some of these marriages are happy, but it is difficult not to wonder if the twenty-five year old woman who is delighted with her fifty-five year old husband will be quite as delighted with him when she is forty – and he is seventy.

On the other hand, to be too dogmatic about age is perhaps to reject a large number of healthy and active individuals. An older person may be much younger in outlook, and even more energetic, than their younger counterparts, who may well be 'over the hill' intellectually, emotionally and sexually, before they have lived half their lives.

Women in their late forties and early fifties can understandably be nervous about entering into a relationship with a man who is much older, for the very unpalatable fact that they are likely to be left alone by the death of their new partner at a time when they themselves are entering a period of their life when it may be very difficult to find another partner. Whether this is realistic or not is beside the point. Few women want to take the risk of spending the last ten or fifteen years of their lives alone.

Vices . . .

Non-smokers often identify themselves and feel very strongly about only meeting other non-smokers. This is very under-standable, as differing views on smoking can often be strong enough to cause arguments. Less often alcoholic consumption is mentioned – the most usual reference is 'drinks socially' or 'occasionally'. Not too many serious drinkers are prepared to admit to it – beware of the potential date who says he or she is in the process of giving up drinking or smoking. They may fail to do either.

. . . and Money

The question of financial status is dealt with in several different ways. The word 'solvent' is used both to describe the advertiser, and the person he or she is seeking. Some rather more hopeful advertisers will say they are seeking 'a million-aire' or 'wealthy wellwisher', but most people will recognize the danger of answering such an overt plea for money in exchange for . . . what? . . . that these advertisements do not tend to attract many replies, unless they are phrased in a very humorous way.

Occasionally an advertisement will be placed by a self-employed person who is looking for a business partner, as well as a potential spouse, and it is easy to understand that a person running a certain type of business from home may not have the time for a social life. But it may also mean that they want to get their money's worth from their advertisement in a different way!

Activities – likes and dislikes

We have looked a little at the words which describe the personalities of advertisers and the people for whom they are looking. But another set of words occurs over and over again, and in some ways it is much more important – that is the set which describes activities, or 'likes and dislikes'. Although this list is not as romantic as the one above, it actually gives much more of a clue to whether the person described is likely to be a suitable partner.

Here are the most frequently occurring activities described:

Music	Walking	Driving	Eating out
Travel	Pubs	Countryside	Cinema
Dancing	Boating	Gardening	DIY
Shooting	Swimming	Theatre	Holidays
Homelife	Reading	Writing	Golf
Antiques	Bridge	Sailing	Various other sports

This seems to make the whole thing very simple indeed! But does it? Let's have a look at a typical advertisement and see what lies behind it.

Professional lady

Mid-thirties, separated. Seeks solvent and sincere gentleman, to share interests. Music, theatre, travel. Car owner. Photo please. All letters answered. Box 777.

Allow this advertisement to conjure up an image for you, before reading on.

Now – here is a little more detail about the lady who

advertised as above. She is a nurse. She has been separated from her husband for four months, and is thirty-seven years old. Her musical favourites are Mantovani, Nat King Cole and the Beatles. She has only been to the theatre twice in the last twenty years, but she enjoyed it so much she is hoping to find someone who 'knows something about it' who will take her again. Her travelling activities in the last four years have been limited to driving eighty miles every weekend to stay with her sick mother. Her mother died six months ago, and that contributed to the breakdown of her marriage, for her husband had been spending these wife-less weekends with his secretary. There is no chance of a reconciliation. Her reason for seeking a 'solvent' partner is that she is hoping to set up an old folks' home.

Perhaps she would have had more suitable replies to her advertisement if it had read something like this:

Professional nurse, 37
Starting own business, would like partner to share pleasures too. Likes driving, Mantovani, Beatles etc. Divorce on the way. Photograph, please. Herts. Box 777.

Let's look at another advertisement.

Keith, 28
Portsmouth, own car and house. Been abroad. Seeks intelligent girl, non-smoker. Many interests. Likes children. Photo please. Box 777.

Can you visualize the man behind this advertisement?

Keith went to live in Australia with his parents when he was eighteen. He had an unhappy marriage; his only child died when three years old and he decided to return to England for a new start. He had a reasonable win on the football pools and has set up his own small printing business. His 'many interests'

23

include tennis and swimming. He is hoping to find a single mother as he would like to share his good fortune with someone in need.

His advertisement is thoughtful, but would have been more explicit if he had said:

Keith, 28

Portsmouth, own car and home. Returned from Australia. Divorced. Non-smoker. Enjoys tennis, swimming. Own business. Seeks intelligent girl, possibly single mother. Box 777.

One 'activity' which deserves a special mention is 'dining out'. This seems to be included in women's advertisements more often than in men's, and not surprisingly gives rise to quite strong feelings when men see it in advertisements. The most frequent criticism of eating out as an activity is that it is *not* an activity at all – it is simply a way of spending quite a lot of money in a very short time. If you are fortunate enough to lead the type of life which includes frequent dining out, and you expect to meet a partner in the same fortunate circumstance, then you are narrowing your field of choice. There is nothing wrong with that, as long as you are aware that most ordinary people – and it must be faced that most people *are* ordinary – do not have the sort of income which allows dining out to be a hobby, rather than an agreeable treat on a special occasion.

Have another look at the advertisements at the end of the previous chapter, and see how much they really tell you about their writers. The aim of the next chapter is to help you to write an advertisement about yourself which says as *much* as possible about you, in the *least* number of words.

Case history: Toby

Being short never bothered me. When I was at school I was

very good at sport, and can't remember anyone ever teasing me about being short. But when I started going out with girls it was another matter. I'm lucky that I'm the sort of person who didn't feel put down by it – I knew I was refused dates because the girl was taller than me – but I told myself that if that was how they judged a person, then they weren't for me anyway.

When I put my advertisement together I thought a lot about whether to mention it or not – and decided I would, but that I wouldn't apologise for it. I can't remember the exact words, but I put something about good things coming in small packages. I thought at least that way I wouldn't have to explain over the 'phone or risk being stood up. Trish was the only girl who said in her reply that a person's height had nothing to do with their worth.

Trish says: I can remember my mother getting very angry when I was little, because someone had said that all short men have oversized egos. It made a great impression on me at the time, not to judge people by their looks. I think I understood what Toby's experiences had been when I saw his advertisement, and I liked the fact that he hadn't let it make him bitter. Anyway, he's taller than me, and that makes us both feel good!

4

Writing Your Advertisement

What to include in your advertisement

The four most important pieces of information that *must* be included in your advertisement are age, sex, marital status and *area*. This last is emphasized, for so many people forget to mention it or think that it is not important. There is nothing worse than having a long correspondence with a 'hopeful' by letter, or telephone, complete with fantasies about love and marriage and moving to live in Edinburgh, or Brighton or somewhere, then actually meeting and finding that you do not click.

Unless you are in search of a relationship that you *want* to keep at a permanent distance, it would be most unwise to try to attract a person who lives more than, say, fifty miles away from you. The apparently brave, who say in their advertisements 'have car, will travel', have either not thought through the possible frustrations of this situation, or perhaps there is something which they are trying to escape – or hide from. You will see later (Chapter 8) how important it is to be able to visit the home of a potential partner before becoming too involved.

It is not always enough to identify only the area in which you live, although there are often reasons for doing this. For example, a person living in Margate will find that by using 'London and South East' or simply 'Kent' as their area identification they will receive far more replies than by using just 'Margate'. This is because of the increase in the number of people living in London who will be attracted. Consider your own means of transport before casting your net too wide, or you will be dependent on the other person to make meetings possible.

The importance of stating age and sex clearly should not

26

need to be explained, but it is surprising how many forget one or the other. Occasionally one finds an advertisement which could have been placed by either a man or a woman. It seems that advertisers may sometimes leave their ages out on purpose, hoping to attract an enormous number of replies. One must assume that they are not particular about the ages of the people they hope to hear from, but the majority of thinking people will not reply to a heartsearch advertisement without knowing the age of the person to whom they are writing.

You may feel strongly enough about the age of a potential partner when you advertise to state limits, such as 'up to', 'about' or 'from'. But, particularly in the upper age groups, you are likely to get replies from older people, even when you are quite explicit about your limits.

Most people will want to know whether you are single, divorced, widowed or married. There is a difference between being 'married' and being 'near-divorced', and a look at some heartsearch columns will demonstrate that some people believe it is quite acceptable to advertise themselves as married, even happily so, but still available for 'fun' or 'casual distraction' or whatever. A 'near-divorced' person *may* still be in a relationship and looking for someone to help them out of it, with all the possible dangers that this may entail.

Many will steer clear of older people (35 plus) who advertise themselves as single. They will make the assumption that the advertiser may have something lacking, that they have stayed at home with 'mum', or are incapable of making an adult relationship. This is, of course, not necessarily so. There are many reasons why a person may not have married, and not all of them should condemn that person to a celibate life. Also, some divorced people may prefer to regard themselves as 'single' rather than 'divorced'.

To help decide what you will put in your advertisement, consider the following.

	Yours	*Partner's*
Age	*	
Area	*	
Sex	*	
Marital status	*	
Height		
Weight		
Occupation		
Eye colour		
Hair colour		
Skin colour		
Nationality		
Children		
Homeowner		
Car owner		
Smoker/non-smoker		
Alcohol consumption		
Religion		
Disabilities		

As already mentioned, the items with a star against them should be considered as absolute priorities to make clear in your advertisement. Look at the other items on the list and make your own decision about whether they are important enough to you – either to advertise about yourself, or to look for in a partner. If they are, tick them, or make a note of them on a separate piece of paper. The items that apply to yourself will form the first part of your advertisement.

Now make a list of all the activities you enjoy. Qualify them where necessary – we have seen that 'music' on its own may be misleading, whereas mentioning the name of a group or a particular composer, leaves no doubt what you are talking about. The same applies to words like 'sportslover'. This can mean anything from watching sport on television, to spending hours on the golf course each day. Be specific. If you are a keen reader, you may like to mention the name of a favourite author; if you're mad about football or cricket, don't be afraid to name the team you support!

When you have completed your list of activities, it may be quite long if you have included everything that you enjoy. Now is the time to edit it. Cross off all the activities that you could *easily* live without. Cross off all the ones that you would like to try, but have never got around to. If you have only dreamed about them, it is possible that there is a very good reason why you have never actually done them, and it is unrealistic to expect to find someone who would 'make' you take part in an activity you have not tackled on your own.

You should end up with three or four activities in which you are actually involved, and which you would find it difficult to do without. It is important to include these in your advertisement, not only because you may find someone who shares your interests, but also because there are some things which though important to you may be quite unpalatable to another person.

Remember Frank, who found his large, cuddly date couldn't stand dogs? There had not been a time in his life when he did not have animals around him, and he had taken them so much for granted it hadn't occurred to him that there are people around who not only have no interest in pets, but actually dislike dogs or cats or budgerigars.

Is this you?

Now you have arrived at the section of your advertisement which deals with the person you are seeking. It is important to remember that the more 'qualifications' you ask for, the more you narrow the field. For example, if you are a young lady of twenty-six, and you mention 'age unimportant', you will receive a vast number of replies. It is likely that many will be from men in their forties, fifties and sixties, so unless you are

29

planning on making a career of collecting 'sugar-daddies', you will set limits. But if you set *strict* limits, then you will not attract many replies at all.

If our twenty-six year old lady seeks a man up to the age of thirty-six, she will receive far more replies than if she gives thirty as the upper limit. If she says she is seeking a husband, she will receive less replies than if she says she is seeking a long-term, or meaningful relationship – though this will not preclude marriage, if the right person comes along.

The advertisements which seem to leave the most people free to answer, are the ones that make the least demands.

Seeks partner, up to 45 years.

or

Seeks friendship with person with similar interests. 47–57 preferred.

or

Would like new start with active widow or divorcee, 60 plus.

Compare the above with:

Seeks warm, unpretentious, slim young lady, preferably blonde who must get on with my children and is not afraid of hard work.

or

I am looking for my dream man who will make me feel like a real woman.

or

Older man seeks younger woman.

Decide now if there is anything of special importance that

you want to add about yourself. Some advertisers mention the starsign under which they were born; still others will add a motto, such as 'Life is too short to waste', or something, which while non-specific, adds a little depth to the advertisement. If humour comes easily to you, use it. Remember that in the few words that you are choosing you are trying to present a picture of a person – not a refrigerator or a secondhand car – so let your final version show something of yourself which is uniquely *you*.

Case history: Jane

I was in a rather silly mood when I wrote my most successful advertisement. I'd been looking at other advertisements for about an hour – just reading them, and they all seemed the same. I thought I'd like to try something different to catch people's eyes, so I started mine off with 'Help! I'm dying of boredom!' Then I put in the usual things about myself, and noticed as I wrote it out that swimming and squash, my favourite things to do, both begin with 's'. After that it was easy – I left the 'help' bit at the beginning, but rewrote the rest starting as many words as possible with an 's'. I had to get the dictionary out, but it was worth it because I had thirty-seven replies to that advertisement – I'd got twelve to the last one, and I think it was because it looked like all the rest. I'm still seeing one of the men who replied. I don't know if anything will come of it, but I certainly don't feel as desperate as I did this time last year.

5

Getting Letters

If you have used *Singles* magazine, you will now have a wait of up to six weeks for your replies, though if you were lucky about the time you posted your advertisement, it may be much less. Be patient, replies will come. Although there is little doubt that *Singles* will reap you the largest number of replies, you may consider placing an advertisement in one of the other journals mentioned in Chapter 2 as this will give you some post to look forward to while you are awaiting your *Singles* responses.

Types of answer: what to expect

Replies will usually fall into one of three categories.

- The long handwritten or typed letter, often with photograph, which will give a great deal of detail about the writer.
- The duplicated letter, which may be a photocopy or, increasingly often, written on a word processor.
- The extremely brief note, usually handwritten and, it seems, invariably from a man.

The short handwritten note

Let's take a look at the third type first. Here's an example:

Why not contact Jim. Slim build, own house, kind and looking for someone just like you.

There will probably be a telephone number, and many women new to the heartsearch industry will respond, as they are intended, to the words 'just like you'. But beware! The experience of many shows that one of the reasons for the brevity of this advertisement is that the writer has tried over and over again *without success* to find a long-term partner, and has given up. Now he is simply trying to get as many women as possible to contact him, with the least effort. Do not feel sorry for him – if he regards the search for a woman in this way, it is likely that there is a very good reason for his lack of success.

You can be almost certain of one thing – if you do telephone him, he will be delighted to hear from you, extremely flattering about you, and will want to arrange a meeting as quickly as possible. If you decide to take this risk do not be surprised to find that he is married, or has other women friends, or that the place where he suggests meeting you is very close to a bedroom.

If you are still intent on meeting the man who writes like this, then perhaps you too are seeking a superficial relationship, and this must be your decision. But remember that while some men find it easy to 'use' women sexually, generally when a woman enters a sexual relationship, no matter how liberated she feels, she will be making some sort of commitment, and can be badly hurt if this is not reciprocated.

The duplicated letter

Moving on to the second type of reply, the duplicated letter, don't be put off by the apparent lack of spontaneity of these respondents. They are putting a great deal of work into their own efforts to find a partner, and you may safely assume that many of them are simply applying their intelligence and industry to the task of telling as many advertisers as they can as much about themselves as possible. But you will have to exercise great and careful judgement about which of these you will choose to follow up, for some of them will have been reduced to using this method out of desperation.

A plea here for the respondents who send stamped, addressed envelopes with their letters. Sometimes these are enclosed with photographs, and a request that you return the photo if you are not interested in taking things any further. At other times you may receive a stamped, addressed envelope simply because the senders have not had much success in their efforts to correspond with others. It is surprising how many people, who may even have promised in their advertisement to 'answer all letters', do not bother with the simple courtesy of using the envelope provided – even to return a photo which can be of no use to them.

Put yourself in the place of someone who has bothered to send out photos, or carefully written letters, gone to the expense of providing a stamp, and still receives little or no response. It does not take a moment to pen a short note of encouragement – you do not even need to include your address – at least you are letting someone know that their letter has arrived, and that you have not thrown it away with no thought.

Here is an example of the duplicated response:

Dear Advertiser

Your advertisement interested me and I think we may have a lot in common.

I have been trying to meet a lady through the medium of advertising for quite some time now, and while I have met a number of people, I still have not found that 'special feeling' which I seek. I hope you will be kind enough to look through the enclosed details about myself, and if you decide that you like the look of me, I would be glad to meet you, or talk on the phone, if you would prefer that.

I have not enclosed a photograph, as I find that it can be quite an expensive process, as many people do not bother to return them, but I would be happy to exchange photos if you wish.

Anyway, good luck with your search, etc. etc.

With this letter, which may be an original or a photocopy, will be a separate sheet with details something like the following:

Joe Bloggs   Address: 2, Ferndale Avenue,
                                                    Crossleigh,
                                                    N. Lincs.
                                          Tel: 0987 65432

Age: 55 years. Widowed three years ago. Two sons, both with own families. Height: 5'9". Hair: plenty, going grey. Eyes: blue. Health: excellent. Non-smoker. Occasional drinker; usually just wine with a meal, if eating out. Printer by trade.

Live on my own in semidetached three-bedroom house. No mortgage! Own a two-year old Volkswagen Polo, two cats and a garden full of flowers and vegetables, depending on the time of year.

My interests are gardening, reading (adventure sagas and travel books). I enjoy going to the cinema – most films, except the ones with very loud pop music. I used to have a dog, and went on lots of long walks; since he died I find I am not walking so much and am thinking about getting another one. There are some lovely walks in this area, if you do not mind getting your boots muddy!

I have worked for the same firm for the last twenty years, and am thinking about taking early retirement. This means that I am not tied to living in this area. I think I would be happy to move if I met a lady who wanted me to share her home, but would not like to be too far away from my sons and their families and hope that a new lady in my life would enjoy my grandchildren (two three-year-olds).

The sort of lady I think I would get on with would be someone who does not expect to be taken out to dinner a lot, as I have learned to cook well since being alone, and prefer to eat in the comfort of my home. She would be a quiet type, who enjoyed walks and evenings at home with a book. I like some programmes on the TV, but do not like to have it on all the time. I do not think I am difficult to live with, but I would like to find someone who would be happy sharing the household jobs. I would not feel good just sitting while a woman did all the work in the house. I think I have been able to manage on my own quite well, and do not want to be dependent on someone, rather to help each other through life, without the loneliness of coming home to an empty house.

I do not think it is possible to make a sudden decision about something as important as living together, or getting married, and so would like to get to know someone over a period of time.

If you think I could be the man for you, please write to me, or telephone me, so that we can begin to get to know each other.

As you can see from the above, Joe has said a good deal about himself. He has given a very good description of his lifestyle, and been open about the type of person he thinks will suit him. He has made no reference to physical type, but wants to exchange photos.

He says that he sees the need to be careful, and to spend time getting to know a potential partner – perhaps he has had the experience of being pushed by someone in the past.

His remark about going home to an empty house is very telling – he is saying that although he wants to retain his independence in a relationship, to have someone to go home to and do things with and for, is very important.

It is unlikely that Joe could have got this amount of detail over to more than one or two people without the help of a photocopier, so the loss of a more personal handwritten letter is balanced by the gain of your learning more about him.

The long handwritten letter

This should need little comment. It will almost certainly be from someone who has not been using the heartsearch columns for very long – a good three-to-four page letter is not something which can be dashed off in a few minutes or repeated over and over again. You will be able to read far more between the lines than with a prepared, typewritten document, for it is bound to be more spontaneous. It may give a far better sense of the person behind the letter.

But – as with presuming that the duplicated letter lacks spontaneity – do not assume that the handwritten letter is always totally truthful and spontaneous. To use the heart-search columns at all, one must be ever conscious that the element of trust is not always well placed. We cannot, nor should we, expect absolute honesty from all contacts, for we all try to present ourselves in the best possible light when we are meeting new people. But there are two types of dis-honesty: the type which is deliberate, and sets out to consciously mislead another, or hide the truth; and the more dangerous type, which is unconscious.

Althea had had more relationships in her life than many people have had hot dinners. She had rejected each and every one of her suitors, or 'gone off them' until they rejected her. When she began to reply to advertisements, she wrote very friendly letters, open and honest, but always used the following words at some point:

I think I have been very unlucky in love, as something always seems to go wrong, no matter how hard I try. I am hoping to find a completely new start with someone who accepts me entirely for what I am. I have a lot to offer the right person.

37

Althea was not being purposely dishonest. That's the way she saw things, and at first glance, she seems to be making a reasonable statement. But consider the words 'who accepts me entirely for what I am'. What Althea really meant is that she wanted to be able to do exactly as she pleased in a relationship. This is not as reasonable as it may sound even in these days of 'doing your own thing'. The most ideal partners have to make adjustments. Even fitting in to each other's daily routine will mean changes for both. There will always be situations in which one or the other has to compromise. Althea's difficulties were not to do with her conscious behaviour – she was a friendly, capable and kind person – and she did have a lot to offer. But when things went wrong, she saw events in very black and white terms. And, in her opinion, *she was always right*.

An American dream: analysing a letter

Dear Advertiser

I hope you don't mind my sending you a photocopied letter! After all, if we two find we are the perfect partners, how we met won't be important, will it?

How does the US of A sound to you? How would you like to spend half the year in your home town in England, and the other half visiting the Grand Canyon, or whooping it up in Hollywood for a weekend?

I can just hear you asking yourself why a lady who has that lifestyle is writing to you in England – hasn't she got everything she wants? The answer to that is no, and I'd give up all I've got to meet the man about whom I fantasize. Why England? I'll tell you.

I was born in the south of your country just before the war, survived the bombings and eventually met and married an American with whom I spent twenty fantastic years on this side of the Atlantic. He died just a few years ago, leaving me well enough off to be able to do the travelling I love so much. Children have flown the nest and are well able to do without their Ma most of the year round.

Every year I visit my relatives in Britain, and over the last few visits I've realized that only an English gentleman could provide me with the sort of warmth and affection I crave. He must have a sense of humour and be free to travel with me.

I have a picture in my mind of what I think this gentleman looks like, and if you don't mind, I'll share it with you.

He would be over thirty years of age, and look something like Edward Fox – I really loved him in the Mrs Simpson series – well-spoken, sophisticated, and very English.

I'm tallish, auburn-haired, slim and look after my appearance. I want a very exclusive relationship. The gentleman might have children, but they will be grown and self-supporting. He should have the same positive outlook which I have – and believe that it's as simple as just replying to my letter with a photograph, to make it all happen.

I'll be visiting your country for three weeks later this year – if you think we might find what we are both looking for, let's get together and get started.

I hope to hear from you.

Mary Smith

A letter like this produces different reactions ranging from 'I hope she finds him!' to 'No wonder she's had to look as far afield as that!'

On the surface, it is just a very optimistic letter from a lady who, it would seem, is prepared to take all kinds of risks to find the man of her dreams. At second glance, taking in the hints she gives about her finances, it is easy to wonder if she will not be deluged with replies from men who would be happy to spend quite a lot of time travelling around America with her.

But when this letter is considered thoughtfully, it is possible to see that the writer has an inner picture or fantasy which is unlikely to be filled in the real world. And this in itself makes the writer vulnerable to the other danger we have discussed – that of attracting a poorly adjusted person who is willing to appear to be this fantasy person, for their own gain.

What does this letter tell the reader about its writer?

First, it suggests, without making a definite statement, that she is well off. She can afford to make frequent trips which many of us would only make once in a lifetime – if we were lucky. She apparently does not need to work.

She is a widow with children, though how many, or their ages, she does not say, except that they are old enough to have left home. She was born in England. She is tall, slim and auburn-haired. She does not tell us how old she is, referring to her birth 'just before the war' which leaves a wide margin for guesses about this important fact.

She says she 'craves' warmth and affection. A strong word to use, suggesting that she may be very lonely indeed – she does not mention a social life, nor activities which bring her into contact with other people, and she makes it clear that she does not want to become too involved with another's family. We may guess that when she says an 'exclusive' relationship is what she wants, she means exactly that. Her reference to her fantasies about the perfect partner could make her very vulnerable – she comes across as a dreamer and that may mean she is ready to trust anyone who seems remotely able to fit into her dreams.

What is she looking for in a partner?

Her guidelines for intending admirers are very narrow – with the exception of age, for she will consider making a relationship with a man up to twenty years younger than herself. She wants to find a very definite physical type, and he must be a typical 'English gentleman' in his speech and behaviour (though the chances of finding 'warmth and affection' in this kind of person may not be high). He should be well off and free from ties – family and work, if he is to fall in with her peripatetic lifestyle. This may attract applications from persons who would be financially dependent upon our seeker, for she does not make any statement about 'solvency'.

Her intention to meet and sift through hopefuls during a three-week visit to England perhaps says more about her approach than anything. Maybe she is *really* looking just for a superficial but 'exciting' adventure. One thing is almost guaranteed; the likelihood of her finding someone who will come close to her Edward Fox image, and being able to check out his integrity during a flying visit from America, is very slim indeed. But no doubt she will have a lot of unforgettable moments trying to make her dreams come true.

Three warnings

Three key attitudes to look for in first letters which should serve as a warning if you find them are:

accusation, *protestation*, *desperation*

People who *accuse* all their previous partners for the failure of their relationship and make only the slightest, if any, claim to responsibility ('Of course, I can see that I must have been partly to blame, *but* . . .') may not have learned to be honest with themselves about the way they interact with others.

People whose letters are *protestations* of their own long-suffering patience and innocence and goodness in the face of the awfulness of life, the dreariness of people generally and the dreadful state of the world, may hold such a negative view that it will take more than a mere human being to dispel their gloom permanently.

41

It is wise to think twice about the *desperate* people who are willing to settle for anything other than loneliness. They may pretend to be whatever suits you, and when you are safely hooked, they will only then begin to allow you to see their true selves – and you may not like that as much as you liked the plastic person you fell for. This is not intended to be unsympathetic about the plight of those who are desperately alone – of course they will try to please. But a firm relationship is not built on the shifting sands of sympathy.

If you find yourself attracted by people who display any of the above attitudes, stop for a moment and question yourself and your own attitudes.

Think about relationships that you have ended. Is it easy for you to point the finger at your ex-partners? How many times have you discarded another person because you did not feel that they were good enough for you, or because they were so far from the high ideals you set for other people? How many times have you felt relieved when a relationship ended, because it meant you no longer had to make an effort to listen to the other's point of view?

Can you take open and honest confrontation of your feelings? How do you feel when another comes to you for help? Helpless, helpful, or powerful? Do you believe that you are a victim of bad relationships, or do you make an honest effort to see how *your* behaviour affects others?

Do you see past partners as people who have been hurt in the break-up of their relationship with you, or just as people who could not adjust to *your* reality? Can you see what their breaking point was, or only your own? Do you always seem to end up with people you think are 'no good' or 'sick', and if so have you ever considered that to be more than a coincidence, and perhaps saying something about yourself?

It may be that your loneliness began with the death of your spouse, and that you have had a happy and fulfilling marriage. Perhaps you are hoping to find the same type of person with whom you have enjoyed the past years. Try to remember that time changes us all and it may be that you will be just as happy with a person who is nothing like your previous partner. Sometimes a surviving spouse experiences guilt that he or she is the one who is still alive, and seeks a 'double' with whom they can resolve this problem. But if you can be aware of this feeling – if it exists – you may find that a quite different personality in your new partner can open new horizons and fresh ways of finding pleasure in your life.

Throughout Celeste's marriage to Morris, they were an active couple, always doing something or going somewhere together. During Celeste's long illness Morris was at first forced to find more home activities, for he did not feel like going out without her, preferring to be with her as much as possible before her death. He began to read all the books that he had never had time to sit down with and developed a love of reading which he now feels will be with him to the end of his days. Now that the period of mourning Celeste's death is over, he is hoping to share his life with a partner who is happier with a much less energetic life than he had previously led. Morris knows that he cannot recreate what he had with Celeste, but he looks forward with hope to the possibilities of the future.

Do relationships always appear to you in black-and-white terms – all good, or all bad? When things begin to go wrong, are you willing to sit down and talk things out, or do you run to your friends, or take a pill, or have a drink, or give up by throwing aside the good things and only acknowledging the bad?

Are *you* 'desperate'? Will you settle for anything, rather than spend a few more weeks or months on your own? Have you ever lived on your own, even for a short while? What sort of experience was it? If your answers to these questions tell you that you are so frightened of being alone that you are willing to turn yourself into a bendy toy to be accepted by another person, then perhaps you would be wise to think

43

about hesitating for a while. Even if you met your ideal partner, in terms of shared interests and intellectual equality, the relationship would be in danger because the fear that you would take into it could blight the commitment you were trying to make. The cripple may be fond of his crutch, but he will always be longing to throw it away.

Case history: Heidi

I really wasn't looking for a close relationship. My marriage had so many problems I thought I would be better off on my own. I did want someone to go out with. But I was so wary that when I answered a number of advertisements I didn't even give my phone number. But Reg did something none of the others managed to do, and I'm still not sure how he did it. He tracked my number down and rang me up. At first I was annoyed – I felt I had a right to my privacy, but he was so nice I decided that it hadn't been such a bad thing after all. We've been together for two years now. . . .

Reg took a risk when he telephoned Heidi – she could have easily been angry about his detective work, but he had made an accurate judgement of her letter – it wasn't that she didn't want to meet anyone, it was that she was frightened to.

6

Making Contact

You have sorted through your replies and decided which of your respondents you think you would like to know a little better. There are three alternatives from which to choose: you can write to them all, sending a photograph if you wish; you can telephone them; or you can use either letter or telephone to arrange an immediate meeting.

Letter writing has one great advantage, and one great disadvantage. The advantage is that two people can exchange a lot of facts about themselves, assuming that their letters are truthful, without leaving the safety of their living room. This may be very pleasant, and the thrill of getting letters can be very romantic.

The great disadvantage is the ease with which it is possible to build a fantasy around a person one has never met. Think again of the imaginary figure of your dreams. The imagination is a very powerful instrument, and it is all too easy to fill in the gaps left by letters with unintentional wishful thinking. We may try to be completely honest about ourselves when we write letters, but we can only reveal a very tiny amount about ourselves and our feelings.

Not what you expected

Many people have been completely disenchanted by the reality of meeting a person with whom they have exchanged letters. This is not to say that disappointment will always be the result, but beware of allowing yourself to become too emotionally involved with a person you have never met.

Terry had answered Claire's advertisement. They lived at opposite ends of the country, and shared a love of the outdoors. Their letters to each other were full of their experiences of the beauties of nature, and each of them began to have daydreams about sharing a sunset, or a particularly beautiful walk, hand in hand. Soon they were discussing in their letters the advantages of living closer together, and both were hinting to their friends that they had found their ideal mate.

At this point they had never even spoken on the telephone, and the most romantic moment occurred when they first heard each other's voice. Both of them later described the events preceding their meeting as 'magical', and admitted that they were so completely carried away by the *idea* of meeting their 'perfect partner' in this way, that they had ignored all the warning signs in each other's letters.

When they finally met, it was a disaster. Neither felt the least attraction for the other. The conversation never got off the ground, and the day that they expected to be the climax of a great love affair turned into an embarrassment for them both.

This is an extreme example, but it highlights the point that *until you actually meet* neither of you will know whether or not that 'special something' is there.

But taking the immediate plunge to meet the prospects of your choice is not always as easy as it should be. It is a fact that many of the people who answer advertisements are not ready to actually meet anyone. They may not be aware of this, and when they first write to you they may have every intention of coming out of their shells. But when it comes to the crunch, they will find a reason to back away. There is little point in putting pressure on a person who feels like this – and their reticence is not your responsibility.

If you have exchanged one or two letters, and are still interested in a prospect, then the next step is a telephone call. Do not wait for the other party to telephone you. If you have exchanged phone numbers, take the initiative and make the call yourself. It can be quite a shock to the system, if you are not used to it, to be the recipient of a social phone call from a complete stranger – bear in mind that while you have had the opportunity to prepare yourself mentally for the event the other party may be taken very much by surprise.

Make it easy: the first phone call

There are ways to begin your phone call that will defuse some of the tension. The first thing to do is to check that you have the right person, and this is especially important if you are making the call to a workplace. There could be great embarrassment if you let the cat out of the bag to a workmate!

When you know you are speaking to your prospect, announce who you are, and identify yourself by making reference to the advertisement, or the letters you have exchanged. Allow a moment to let this news sink in, then ask if it is a convenient time to telephone. There are moments in everyone's life when a call from a complete stranger could be embarrassing! If the answer is 'no', do not be afraid to ask if it is all right for you to ring at another time, and ask for a specific time to do so.

At this point you may sense that your call was not really welcome. There is no need to become hurt or angry about that, but if you do feel it very strongly, put the ball back in the other person's court by asking if he or she would prefer to ring you. Their reply to that should give you a better idea of whether they really want to take things any further.

Many people become discouraged if they are rejected on a first phone call. Don't be. It says more about lack of intent on the other person's part than it does about you or your desirability. I repeat: *you will find that some people are only able to get as far as first base with this method of meeting people, because they lack the confidence in themselves to continue.*

Let's assume you have managed to make a telephone contact. It will be tempting at this stage to do away with all patience and suggest, or agree with a suggestion, that you should arrange a meeting. Think twice. There are many things that you may want to know about this person before you decide that a meeting is a good idea.

Try not to give way to the fear that this is your one and only chance of a date. It isn't. You are looking for a person with whom you may want to spend the rest of your life. There are many more people out there whom you can meet in exactly the same way as you have met this one. There is no need for haste, and you will find that meetings can turn out to be a waste of time – and money – if you say 'yes' to everyone who asks you out.

Talking on the telephone to a person you have not met may not be the easiest thing you have done, but remember that the other person probably feels the same. And it is a lot easier than actually meeting a complete stranger with *no* previous conversation.

Perhaps the simplest way of putting both of you at ease on this very important call is to simply express your feelings, and ask if they are shared by the other person.

I feel a bit nervous about talking to someone I haven't met. Have you done this before?

Make it clear what you expect from this phone call. It can be surprisingly hard to get a conversation off the ground if neither knows what the other is expecting.

I thought if we talked a bit on the phone, we'd get an idea if we were likely to get on together.

Acknowledge that you have read and digested the letter that led to this phone call.

I know you like cricket – do you play or watch?

The thing I really liked about your letter was that you said you enjoyed poetry – I wondered who your favourite poet was?

Most lonely people welcome the chance to talk to another person. If a conversation gets out of balance, one person will be doing all the talking and the other all the listening. If you find that you are doing all the talking – not because you have the need to, but because the other person seems reluctant to say much – then make room for them to talk. It is quite easy to change the balance by asking a question, and then just keeping quiet, so that the other person has time to reply. If he or she pauses, it may be a temptation for you to start again, but you will usually find that if you bite your tongue at this point, and allow a silence, the other person will eventually say something.

Remember that many people find it difficult to speak easily about themselves, and need space and encouragement to do so.

If you are the one who seems to be doing all the listening – is it because there is no space for you to say anything, or because you are reluctant to make a contribution to the conversation? If it is the former you will need to make your own judgement of the person who is doing all the talking. Could they be just reacting nervously to the situation, or are they a person who is so engaged with their own experience of life that they do not recognize another person's need to express themselves. Or is he or she just not interested in another's point of view?

Wendy telephoned Dave in reply to his letter. She was overwhelmed by the flow of words that he fired at her. He described his house in minute detail, including colours of curtains and carpets. Wendy's first reaction was that he was boasting and trying to impress her with his material assets, and she decided that someone who thought belongings as important as he evidently did could not be the kind of person she

49

would get on with. But there seemed to be no stopping him, short of putting the telephone down in mid-sentence.

In the end she decided to be quite honest and said 'Stop!'. There was an awkward silence, then she told him kindly that she felt he was far more interested in 'things' than she was, and he would probably be bored with her company as she was very non-materialistic. She said she would be happy in a mud hut – with the right person.

Later that evening Dave telephoned Wendy and apologized for the way he had 'gone on' about his house. He explained to her that he found talking to new people difficult, and he would like to try again – without mentioning carpets or curtains. Dave had been impressed by Wendy's honesty, and she was impressed by his willingness to try again. They eventually met and found that they shared a lot of interests.

If you have negotiated a first telephone call and are still interested in the person, instead of arranging a meeting it is a good idea to ask them to telephone you in a couple of days. This will give you the time to reflect a little on your feelings when the first flush of enthusiasm has died away. It will give you a chance to test the other's interest and reliability by putting the ball back in their court. And, quite importantly, when you have made the first approach, it will take you out of the role of pursuer – a necessary role from time to time, but not *all* the time!

Do not be afraid of telephone calls – making them or taking them. The telephone is an excellent way to learn about yourself, as well as your potential partner. If there is something worrying you about the other person, the telephone is the first place to learn that it is all right, in the heartsearch game, to ask questions which would be regarded as a little forward under other circumstances. If there is anything that is being hidden or ignored that you can discover by a straightforward question on the phone – take the risk. It will be better than being disillusioned after you have met, and begun to be involved with the whole person, rather than just a voice on the phone.

More than one heartsearcher has felt the need to say:

> I know I shouldn't have to ask this, but I have a feeling that you are still married, or living with someone?

and received an answer in the affirmative. It is a fact of life that while it takes a special kind of person to tell outright lies about their circumstances, there are many who believe that simply omitting to share an important piece of information is not dishonest. They can always use the excuse that 'you never asked them'. There are plenty of honest people out there waiting to meet you. If you have doubts, make every effort to check them out.

But if you are a person who has real difficulty in communicating on the telephone, take heart, for it is not the only way to begin a new relationship – as Charles discovered.

Case history: Charles

I don't know if it was something to do with how I came over on the phone or if I was just unlucky to start with. I seemed to be always getting my hopes up about someone I'd spoken to a few times, then when I asked her out suddenly she wouldn't be available, and I'd lose touch.

I decided to change my approach. I began to write one-page letters in reply to adverts – telling the basic details about myself, and the fact that I wanted a lasting relationship. But I said I wasn't interested in talking on the phone, because I believed we could only really get to know each other by meeting. At first I didn't have much success – I suppose some people could have seen my letters as aggressive, but I kept trying and eventually June wrote back and said she agreed with my view, and we met without talking on the phone at all.

The first few minutes were a bit strained, then one of us – I can't recall which – said something funny, and from then on it was as though we'd known each other all our lives. We're both in the same line of business and I suppose we need to be pretty aggressive to be successful. But we get on fine, and that's what matters.

7

Meeting: Where, When and Why

By now you may be feeling very excited and believe that you are set for some outings, a widening of your social life, or you may already be wondering whether to have a church wedding or not. Don't worry if you feel your imagination is making unwonted leaps and bounds with very little reason. You are certainly not the first to do that.

Most people's natural need for companionship and security will have them hoping they are close to finding what they seek. There is nothing wrong with this, and it will enable you to meet prospective partners in a positive frame of mind. But try to differentiate between the fantasy of success in love, and the reality of your situation. You are about to meet some people who have, as you did, presented you with their best behaviour and who want to get on with you. But it might not happen. When you actually meet, you may be disappointed to find that you just do not 'click'.

This can be very discouraging, particularly if you have pinned all your hopes of meeting someone on your advertisement. Also, you might be tempted to become involved with someone who is really not your type, or about whom you have many doubts, rather than return to the no-hope situation in which you may have been a few weeks earlier.

If you have found the process of dealing with the results of your advertisement an exciting or pleasant one, now is the time to think about placing another advertisement. This will give you something to look forward to, and cushion you should you discover that your first advertisement has not found you an appropriate partner. By now you may also have a much more realistic idea of what is involved in using this method to meet people. You will undoubtedly want to take a good look at the advert which you used, and will find that no matter how much care you put into it, there will be changes to make in your presentation of yourself and your hopes.

Assuming that you are now ready to meet a prospect from your first advertisement, there are number of things to consider about this meeting.

First meetings: taking care

Nowadays it is quite acceptable for the suggestion for a meeting to come from a woman, although not all men will welcome that. Many women feel more comfortable if they are invited out by a man for despite the ability of modern women to be more independent than their grandmothers were, many of them still perceive their role in the marriage stakes as the pursued, not the pursuer. Most women will feel humiliated if they are left to make all the going, unless they are in search of a man who prefers to be taken charge of by a woman.

But no matter who does the 'asking' – and when the date is the result of an advertisement it is often just a natural happening – both should have an equal say about where and when the meeting should take place.

If the meeting goes well, and the two people involved find that they are enjoying one another's company, it hardly matters where they are, for they will no doubt be able to make decisions together about how long the meeting will last, and whether there will be other dates.

But life is not always as obliging as that, and painful situations can arise when the two do not attract each other as they had hoped they would.

Ralph was very casual about first meetings. He would ask the lady in question what she would like to do.

Almost invariably they would suggest a meal in a restaurant, and to start with that seemed the polite and civilized thing to do. But I did not meet the lady of my dreams for some time, and when I look back at the number of hours I spent sitting bored out of my mind, listening to the history of someone's broken marriage, or their financial troubles, I only wonder what made me persevere. And I spent a fortune on meals. The last straw was a woman who talked non-stop about the Chelsea Flower Show for an a hour and a half – and I haven't even got a garden.

Bella had the same experience, in a different way.

I'm mad keen on being out of doors, and I met a whole succession of men who suggested that we go for a walk somewhere. I had the feeling eventually that they wanted to see what I was like before they invited me for a meal or something. Unfortunately they often seemed to have a better opinion of me than I had of them. I happen to be a very good listener, and I can't tell you how many hours I spent doing just that. I used to start looking at my watch and inventing all sorts of ludicrous excuses for having to cut short a walk. The last time this happened I had spent three solid hours wandering around Hyde Park listening to the second world war experiences of a man who had knocked about ten years off his age. His last words to me were that he could never be bored with a person like me. But I'd been bored stiff!

This is not to condemn Bella's world war two veteran. Somewhere there is a woman who would be fascinated to hear his experiences, but it is not Bella. Both Bella and Ralph learnt to make some rules about first meetings which helped them to avoid the traps into which they had fallen.

Here are some suggestions about first meetings:

- Avoid a meeting that involves the spending of money on meals, etc., unless there is a clear understanding that you are 'going Dutch'. (This does not preclude a cup of coffee, or a drink.) As soon as one person has paid for a meal it is almost impossible for the other not to feel some sense of obligation, and it can be awkward to refuse a second date with a person who has just paid for an expensive meal.

- Make it clear that you expect the first meeting to last only an hour. This is not as difficult as it sounds. You can either tell your date with complete honesty that you would prefer a short first meeting to give both of you the opportunity of deciding whether you will arrange further dates; or you can arrange that first meeting at a time when you must get away after an hour or so, for some other appointment or event. The first alternative may be harder if you are not very sure of yourself, but it has the advantage that if you do get on very well, you can change your mind and spend more time together, by mutual agreement.

- It is extremely wise to avoid a first meeting in the home of either one of you. There are many completely trustworthy people into whose home you could safely go, and these same people would not abuse your trust if you invited them into your home. But a first meeting on neutral ground can be terminated at will by either party. This is not the case if one is invited into the intimacy of another's home.

- Avoid meetings which involve either of you being taken somewhere in the other's car. Apart from the obvious dangers, particularly to a woman, in putting yourself entirely in the hands of a stranger in this way, there is the very simple fact that as soon as you become a passenger in another's vehicle, you have surrendered a good deal of control over your situation. Again, in a trusting relationship, you must be able to do this from time to time, but the first date is *not* the time to begin.

- Avoid theatres and cinemas – sitting next to someone in the dark will not teach you much about them. Many people would say that a film or a concert is an ideal icebreaker, and perhaps if you have great difficulty becoming involved in a conversation with a new person, this may serve to put the moment off for a couple of hours. But a relationship cannot begin in earnest until the people involved are ready to sit down, look at each other and share their thoughts and feelings.

That first hour

There are many ways to spend that first hour with a prospective partner, and each person will have different ideas, depending on their likes and dislikes. Perhaps you would like to use that hour to do something you haven't done before, or have enjoyed in the past but have not done for some time.

Gwen and Guy met in the park. Gwen brought sandwiches, and Guy brought a flask of coffee. They can't remember whose idea it was, 'it just seemed to happen that way', but they still walk to the same park on fine evenings and it has become a little piece of their 'family history'.

Denis and Pauline met outside one of the great cathedrals, intending to go for a short walk. It began to pour with rain and though neither of them were church members, they took the simplest solution and wandered round the cathedral. As well as saving themselves from a soaking they discovered that they shared a deep love of history and a non-conventional religious belief.

A more unusual story is told by Gavin:

I had been writing to Diane for about six months – and we had been talking on the telephone a lot. She lived in Durham, and I had been in London for a couple of years, although I grew up in Somerset. We got on well enough to have discussed our feelings about the possibility of meeting, and not getting on as well as we did at a distance. We dithered a lot about meeting because we were both frightened to lose what we had. Then I lost my job. I wasn't too hard up and I knew I could get work anywhere so I decided to take the plunge and visit Diane.

I have close relatives in Scotland, and I arranged to spend some time there, then call in on Diane on the way back South. To cut a long story short, I never made it back to London. What was to be a meeting between trains in the station buffet at Durham turned into lunch, then a long walk, then I was looking for a bed and breakfast, and Diane was preparing her parents to meet me. . . .

Gavin found work in Durham as he had predicted and he and Diane are now settled down in their own home.

The approach

You have made your first date. You have probably checked, with a little humour, how you will recognize each other. No matter how many times you meet people using this method it is unlikely that you will be able to approach a meeting without a mixture of pleasure and apprehension. Most of the pleasure is a natural reaction to the idea of a new person in your life who is interested enough in you to want to meet you, together with the pleasantly romantic hope that this meeting could lead to a long and positive relationship – perhaps marriage and a whole new life.

For most people the apprehension comes from two sources; simply stated they are 'Will *I* like *them?*' and 'Will *they* like *me?*' Whichever of these two questions is the most important to you will depend on how much you like *yourself*! Try to work towards an attitude of 'Will *we* like *each other?*' and recognize that the absence of appreciation by another person does not necessarily mean there is something wrong with you, but more often they are just not the right person. Being prepared to find acceptance is as important as being prepared for rejection.

One of the most hurtful things that you can do at this stage is to stand your date up. This may be true of any date, but remember how you are feeling about taking a step in the dark towards another person; imagine how you would feel if they simply did not bother to turn up. If for any reason at all you are unable to keep the appointment you have made, try to find a way to let them know. If that is impossible, leave a message, or contact them as soon as possible afterwards and explain what happened. Most people will accept a reasonable explanation, and it may be possible for you to arrange another meeting.

But, no matter how nervous you feel about walking up to a stranger and saying 'Are you John, or Mary, or whoever?' – just *DO IT*.

Paul had arranged to meet Teresa. He was an extremely shy man and had found the whole business of answering advertisements difficult. This was the first time that he had screwed up enough courage to actually ask a woman out by this means. He was a widower who had experienced many years of quiet contentment with his wife. He was sick of living on his own. Teresa did not turn up, but while he was waiting for her Paul had noticed a woman looking at him. He wondered if it was Teresa, but as she was not wearing the red coat by which he was to recognize her he did not approach her.

Paul waited for an hour before going home. He felt awful. He was sure that the woman had been Teresa – that she had decided she did not like the way he looked, and so not bothered to speak to him. It may be that Teresa was the loser, for Paul was a gentle and loving man with a lot to offer the right partner. Teresa's non-appearance said more about her than it did about Paul. No matter how nervous she was, and even if there was something about Paul's appearance that she could not accept, it would not have cost her anything to have greeted him and spent a few minutes with him, even if she then used an excuse to cut the meeting short.

Even so, it is understandable that you should have a few butterflies in your tummy when the moment comes, particularly if it is the first time you have ever met anyone this way. Unless you have seen a very good photograph of the person you are meeting, their appearance will seldom fit with the picture you have made of them in your imagination. The temptation to crack a joke at this point has been known to fall flat. Vicky walked up to the man in the black raincoat and said, 'I feel as though I'm picking up a complete stranger!' Unfortunately she was, for the wearer of this black raincoat was waiting for his wife! Vicky retired, confused and embarrassed, but at least she had a story to break the ice when the right raincoat arrived.

The simplest approach is the one least likely to cause embarrassment. 'Are you Mary Jones', delivered with a smile can only produce a 'Yes' or a 'No', and if you have been careful enough to describe each other's appearance there is not much that can go wrong. Many people find the first few minutes of a meeting a bit of an anticlimax. Instead of the hoped-for instant romantic gratification, suddenly one is faced with what can be an awkward social situation. Unless you have made definite plans to go somewhere, or do something, you may find yourself walking aimlessly along a street, each wondering what the other wants to do. This can easily be the result of meeting at a railway station. It is easier to overcome the first few minutes if you are sitting down, and therefore have to make an effort to break the ice. That is why so many first meetings take place in coffee bars, on park benches, or in pubs.

Question time

Do not be afraid to ask questions at this meeting. You both need to find out certain things about each other, and only by asking questions will you get answers. You will also open the way for the other person to question you. You can learn as much about them from their questions as from their answers. Is a lot of interest being shown in you, and your likes and dislikes? Are the questions about material things perhaps aimed at finding out more about your financial situation? How do you feel about the situation? Is the atmosphere between you friendly, or do you feel as if you are being interviewed for a job? When you ask a question, do you feel you get a clear and straight answer, or that things are being concealed? Does the answer go on and on until the question has been forgotten? Is there *balance* in the conversation, or is it one-sided?

It sometimes happens in a strange situation, that you find you cannot stop talking. If you are the sort of person who likes to talk a lot anyway, and you really need a good listener, then it doesn't matter too much. What your new partner is seeing is the real you, and it is their decision whether or not they want to be your listener. But if you find that you are talking fifteen to the dozen because of nervousness, there is only one thing to do: *STOP!*

Take a deep breath and say something like 'Sorry! I don't usually go on like this. I think I must be nervous!'

Then be as strong as you need to be to give the other room to talk. Keep up your determined effort. Don't allow yourself to interrupt. If there are silences, you needn't always be the one to end them by speaking. Some of the most meaningful revelations are made as the result of the reflection that is allowed by a silence.

I'll be seeing you . . .?

Remember the value of a smile. Even if you are finding yourself stressed by the situation, a smile will do wonders, not only for yourself, but for your partner. Imagine how you feel if you are confronted by an anxious face – your own anxiety may begin to rise. But if the face in front of you looks cheerful, it is easier for you to respond. The same is true for your partner, and your smile will be an invitation for them to share something pleasant with you, instead of worrying about whether you like them or not.

Whatever the circumstances of your first meeting, you must make a decision about whether there will be a second. It is not always a good idea to make this decision until you have had time to consider your feelings about your prospect. If you have been deprived of close human contact for some time, or suffered the pain of an unsuitable or failing relationship, the temptation to ignore negative feelings about another person will be very great. Do not forget that many of the divorces which are granted each year are the results of people rushing to the altar a second time, perhaps on the rebound, perhaps out of sheer desperation to accept *anything* to avoid loneliness.

Do not deceive yourself with the idea that it is easy to leave a relationship that is going bad. *It can be extremely difficult.* If it were easy to walk out on an attempted commitment to someone, then there would be no such thing as a broken heart, and no pain in breaking off. Every day that you delay jumping in at the deep end could be a week of tears saved later.

Give consideration, also, to the other party. It is most unfair to lead another person to believe that he or she is beginning a meaningful relationship with you when that is not the case. Again the word balance springs to mind. You may have very strong feelings at this stage, but they could be due to the simple relief that you *may* have 'found what you are looking for'. In these early days let reason have as much say as heart.

No matter how enthusiastic you feel on that first date, consider making just one rule for yourself: *before arranging a second date, stand well back and reflect on your feelings about this new person in your life.*

This is a most important time. If the other person is truly interested in you, he or she will not push you. You should be able to say, if asked for a date:

I've really enjoyed meeting you. I think I'd like to see you again. But I would like a little time to think about things. Would you mind if I gave you a call tomorrow?

62

It may be that the next day you will rush to the telephone to let them know you can't wait to see them again. Or perhaps when you get home you decide that you are not ready to take another person seriously. You may remember things about the day that you did not enjoy; maybe there were times when you did not feel free to express yourself openly. The simple fact that you have been out with a completely new person, and now have the choice whether or not to continue the relationship has taken you to a new crossroads in your life. Pause before you decide which turning to take.

Case history: Lucy

Ted and I have been talking about getting married. Before I met him I found it hard to believe that I would ever meet anyone apart from the people I worked with. I got on well with them, but somehow my social life never got off the ground. When I reached my twenty-fifth birthday I got really worried. Most of my dates had been with guys at work, and I think I only went out with them because they were there, not because I felt particularly attracted to them. I suppose I'd made the choice to put my career before my social life. The first few times I spoke to Ted on the phone I didn't really take the whole thing very seriously. I'd answered a few advertisements for something to do more than anything else. I never thought it would come to anything. When he first suggested meeting I got quite scared – a voice on the phone was one thing, but to actually go out with a man I knew nothing about – that was a different matter.

In the end I told my mum about it – I was still living at home. I was a bit surprised when she encouraged me to go! She said she'd been wracking her brains to think of ways I could meet new people . . . that was something I hadn't known! I rang Ted back and said I'd like to meet him. He was surprised; he thought he'd put me off in some way.

I told mum I'd only be gone for an hour or so, because I still felt the whole thing was a bit of a joke, but I had to phone her half way through the evening because we got on so well I didn't get home till just after midnight.

Ted told me later he'd had to screw all his courage up to ask me out because he thought I'd say no – and he'd rather have just had a telephone relationship with me than none at all. Which is a pretty nice thing for a man to say, isn't it?

8

Winners and Losers

No matter where you meet a prospective partner – at a party, at work, or perhaps through a friend or relative – there is no guarantee that you are meeting the answer to all, or even some, of your dreams. But when you meet someone in the normal course of your life, you will probably have mutual friends, and because of this there will be things that you are told about your new acquaintance, or ways in which you can easily check the truth of what they tell you about themselves. This is simply *not* so when you meet someone through an advertisement – it cannot be emphasized enough that you only know what you are told, *or what you take the trouble to find out for yourself.*

Case histories

The following stories are true, although the names and circumstances of the people involved have been changed to protect their privacy. They are to underline for you the importance of not always taking things at their face value, but also to illustrate that, with a little luck, you may find the ideal partner for your own personal situation and needs.

Marion – blinded by love

It is not only sensible, but *imperative* to check basic facts about people. If Marion had not been so trusting of Richard, she would have avoided a lot of emotional pain.

Marion had lived overseas for some years, and when she returned to this country, she had lost touch with most of her family. She placed an advertisement in a heartsearch column and had several replies. Only Richard's really interested her, for his letter stood out from the rest with its unusual sense of humour. She was enthusiastic about meeting him, but at first he seemed reluctant. He telephoned her once or twice, and she understood that he lived in a bedsitter and had been divorced for some years.

At first he seemed suspicious of her. This put her on the defensive, and made her all the more determined to prove that she was unlike his wife, whom he told her had behaved so badly towards him that he had had a breakdown. He said he now found it very difficult to trust women.

When after a few weeks they did meet, Marion fell instantly for him, for he displayed the most charming and romantic behaviour she had ever encountered. He seemed to reciprocate her feelings, and within a very short time, Marion thought she had found the answer to all her fears of a lonely future. She became so enraptured by Richard's way of spinning a private little world for the two of them that she did not think it important that they seldom, if ever, met in the company of other people.

Richard began to spend weekends with Marion – he lived too far away to visit her during the week – and though Marion had spare time, he said his landlady did not like him having visitors. Marion did not question this.

He admitted he was not well off – Marion owned her own home, and appreciated the help he gave her with decorating, etc. He telephoned her one evening and said that he had been made redundant, and that he would no longer be able to make the weekend visits which she now depended upon so much. She immediately sent him enough cash to fill the tank of his car with petrol, and the following weekend declared that she could help him to pay off his current debts, amounting to £300 or £400. This she did. She was quite sure that he would soon suggest moving in with her, and was shattered when a couple of weeks later he telephoned her to say that he was finding the relationship stressful and was 'dropping out of sight' for a few days.

She did not hear from Richard for two weeks, then he phoned her again, as though nothing had happened. By now Marion's attachment to him was too strong to be thrown off easily, and she began to make excuses to herself for his sometimes erratic behaviour. The stories he had told her about his wife's infidelities, and the way in which she had hurt him, had called up Marion's maternal instincts, and she was determined that she would not let him down.

It took over a year of sudden inexplicable disappearances, and constant changes of Richard's mind about the relationship and whether or not it had a future, before Marion was prepared to admit to herself that she was involved with a person who just did not behave normally. There had been times when Richard's mood had changed so dramatically that she was left feeling as though she was with another person altogether. She knew he had spent some time in a hospital with his 'breakdown', but somehow the way he described it, it seemed that the doctors were the sick people and Richard the only sane one.

Marion's words:

> Perhaps the penny would have dropped more quickly if he had not been so marvellous when he was 'all right'. We had a terrific holiday together (which I paid for, of course) when he didn't put a foot wrong. Of course, I wanted to believe that the rest of the world was at fault, because that would have meant that there was nothing wrong with him.

The final heartbreak came when Marion, having not heard from Richard for several days, decided to visit him at his home. She was shocked to find that although it was true that Richard lived in rented accommodation, it was not in the bedsitter he had described. He had the run of his landlady's house. He had lived with her for over ten years and she did everything for him, from cooking to handwashing his underwear, and keeping his room tidy. He was also dependent on her for money, as he had not worked for six years, despite what he had told Marion about losing a job. Also, his absences were explained. He attended the local psychiatric hospital as a day patient, and every couple of weeks his behaviour would become so bad that he was admitted for a few days. He had a history of psychiatric illness which went back to his childhood.

Marion again:

> His landlady was most concerned when she realized how deeply I had become involved with him. If I'd been sensible, I'd have insisted on seeing his 'home' before becoming committed to him. He couldn't possibly have hidden his circumstances or the state of his mental health from me then. But I'm more angry with myself for being bowled over by someone whom I really knew nothing about – and by the time I did know the truth, I was so deeply in love that it took me months to get over him and to trust myself to get involved with someone else.

Penny – a success story

Penny was the mother of two small children. She was divorced and struggling with a job to try to make a decent home for them. Most of the people she met at work were married, and she felt very self-conscious about the fact that her marriage had 'failed'. She had been asked to go out once or twice by the few unmarried men she came into contact with, but was very aware that as soon as they found she had children, they lost interest. The fact that she had to find babysitters, and pay for them from her tight budget, did not help matters when it came to spending an evening out.

Penny had almost decided to stop thinking about having a 'man in her life' when her sister persuaded her that advertising for a partner was not a bad thing to do. Until then, Penny had seen advertising as a last resort, only used by people who had 'something wrong' with them. But when she began to look at heartsearch columns seriously she noticed that many of the advertisements she read included the phrase 'likes children', so she decided to try her luck.

She started by answering advertisements placed by men a few years her senior, and did not pay a great deal of attention to what they seemed to be seeking. She became disheartened when she found that many of the men to whom she wrote seemed to be reluctant to meet her, though they were quite willing, at the beginning, to have long telephone calls, often at her expense. Penny began to suspect that they wanted someone to talk to, but were not willing to take any of the responsibilities of a meeting, or what it might lead to.

Eventually, Penny decided to place her own advertisement, and she gave the wording a great deal of thought. The response pleased her, as her advertisement had been open about the fact that she was a mother, and that her children were important to her. This also meant that when she got to the point of actually meeting one or two of the men, there was no embarrassment about telling them that going out in the evenings was not as easy for her as it would be for a woman with no children.

She soon found that in her case having children was an advantage, for she met Bruce who had lost contact with his own children when his wife had illegally removed them from the country during divorce proceedings. Penny says: 'She must have been mad – he is a natural father. My two took to him so well, that when we went out together people often thought that he *was* their father.'

Penny and Bruce are planning to marry in the near future, and both of them realize that they would not have met without the medium of advertising, for they are both quiet people who do not feel at ease at parties or in pubs. Neither of them lived in the area in which they grew up, and this made it even more difficult for them to find a social circle. Bruce had been heartbroken by the loss of his own children, and can't believe that Penny's two have accepted him so easily.

Adrian – taken for a ride

Adrian's tale is not such a happy one. Although he was in his early thirties his shyness had prevented him from ever having a relationship which went beyond a first or second date. His mother had been sick for as long as he could remember, and he had devoted much of his time to looking after her, particularly since the death of his father.

He picked up a copy of a magazine one day and saw an advertisement placed by Celia. He liked the idea of meeting her, for she had three children. Adrian had never seen himself as having children, but the idea of stepping into a family which had lost its own father appealed to him.

His first meeting with Celia overwhelmed him. She was an extremely attractive woman, and the way she treated him made him feel a little like Cary Grant, for she was flattering and admiring. Within a short time he had taken her home to meet his mother, towards whom Celia behaved with great kindness.

Celia told Adrian that she owned her own home, and that she had been abandoned two or three years earlier by her husband, who, while she was careful not to criticize him openly, came across as an uncaring person. She was older than Adrian, but he ignored that – what did a few years matter when he felt as though he was making up for all the wasted time?

Adrian proposed to Celia only two months after their first meeting. He was overjoyed at her acceptance, and agreed with her suggestion that he move into her home. He arranged a live-in companion for his mother.

Adrian was not a poor man. As a successful businessman, he had been able to make various investments, and had learned to manage his money very well. He offered to pay for the redecoration of Celia's house before their wedding, for he saw her as someone who had suffered financially as the result of her husband's behaviour, and he was eager to try to make up for it.

The crunch came after the wedding. From the very first day, it seemed to Adrian that Celia was not the same woman who had made him feel so good before. Nothing he did seemed to be right, and Celia was snappy and miserable. After only a few weeks, their relationship had deteriorated so badly that Adrian was beginning to prefer working late to coming home.

Then, after a particularly bad argument Celia told Adrian she had not been honest about her finances and that the house was heavily mortgaged; she was behind in her payments, and had been afraid to tell him.

Adrian was appalled, thinking that he was somehow at fault for taking things so much for granted. He told her that as he was her husband it was only right he should pay out the mortgage. They could 'start again' without the burden of worry that Celia had been carrying on her own.

Things seemed to improve after Adrian had carried out his promise. But not for long; Celia's first husband reappeared and she did not seem to mind his arriving unannounced whenever he felt like it. Eventually, before Adrian and Celia had been married even six months, the atmosphere in the house became so unbearable, he decided to move back to his mother's home.

In Adrian's own words:

It slowly filtered through to me that I had been taken for a complete idiot, which I suppose I was. I was in far too much of a hurry to get married. Now that I look back on it I can see how unrealistic I was. I suppose I had never met a woman who could make me feel so good before. If I had taken a bit of trouble – got to know Celia's neighbours, for example, I would have found out that her ex-husband had been a regular visitor ever since their divorce. It's now obvious to me that most of their problems were money worries – neither of them had a clue about how to manage money, and all I did, in the long run, was to solve the biggest problem of all – paying off the mortgage. *I do not believe that any of this was planned. It just happened.* They are still not back together, or anything like that, but it's clear to me that I have learned a very expensive lesson about human nature – and about myself.

Adrian has decided not to take any more risks. He estimates the cost of his 'lesson' at more than £20000, and has not yet decided whether he will bother to take action to get any of his money back.

Helen – a friend in need

Helen was just getting over a relationship which had turned sour. She answered an advertisement placed by a man who lived in the west country. She knew that she was not in a position to move so far away from her job, but after an exchange of letters she began to feel more than a little interest in Douglas, particularly as his marriage had just broken up and he seemed to be suffering from the same sense of loss that she was experiencing. Against the advice of her friends and family, she decided to accept an invitation to spend two weeks of her annual holiday with Douglas at his home.

Douglas had his own small business to run, and Helen fell easily into the routine of cooking his meals during the day. He finished work early while she was staying with him, and they enjoyed long walks in the afternoons. Douglas insisted on taking Helen out to dinner every evening, saying it was the least he could give her in exchange for her company.

In Helen's words:

Douglas was great. He seemed to understand that I wasn't

ready for a close relationship, and during that two weeks we got to know each other as friends. We realized that while we got on well together on that level, neither of us felt physically attracted to the other. The result was that we had a chance to help each other regain a certain amount of faith in human nature – something we had both been in danger of losing as the result of a bad break-up with our previous partners. After I returned home we wrote to each other a few times. Then he met someone else, and so did I. I'll never forget his kindness and understanding, and we'll probably always go on exchanging Christmas cards.

I'm glad we didn't live closer to each other, as I think we would both have been tempted to make more of the relationship than it would stand. As things were, I really had to think hard about what I wanted – and what I was willing to give.

Dave – a misunderstanding

Dave's one love was serious music – by which he meant Mozart, Beethoven and Sibelius. His wife had only liked pop and this had caused quite a lot of problems. So when Dave decided to advertise for a partner, the first thing he put in his advertisement was 'serious music lover'. He had a number of replies but, with the exception of one, none of them mentioned music of any kind as an interest. The exception, Jennie, wrote that music was her chief interest, too, and that she had no time for pop. Dave and Jennie exchanged a number of letters, and Dave decided that there were a lot of other things about Jennie which he liked. He telephoned her to arrange a date.

Let Dave continue:

She sounded so nice when I spoke to her. We arranged to meet, and I was feeling very good about the way things were going. Just before I put the phone down, she asked me if I had watched a country and western concert on television the night before. Then she was telling me how much she had enjoyed it, and how it was so much better than pop music.

I felt dreadful. It was obvious that her idea of serious music was as different from mine as chalk is from cheese, and I knew it would be a waste of time meeting her. I tried to talk a bit about my kind of music, but she hadn't even heard of most of the composers I love. I sat down straight after the phone call ended and wrote to her, making an excuse. I hope I didn't hurt her feelings, but it seemed better than letting things go on, and I wouldn't dream of standing someone up.

After that I gave a lot of thought to the importance of music to me, and I decided that I really couldn't get on with someone who didn't have the same tastes. The next advertisement I put in, I actually named the composers I like, so there was no mistake. I didn't get as many answers, but at least they were all on my wavelength.

Patricia – a lucky escape

Patricia was staying with a friend in London when she placed an advertisement looking for a lasting relationship, but she owned a house in Bournemouth where she spent some of her weekends. Because of the nature of her work she found it extremely difficult to meet new people, and she was delighted when she had a reply from a man who said he lived in Bournemouth, but spent time in London when he was travelling in his occupation as a journalist.

The first few letters that they exchanged left her feeling very hopeful. Peter seemed to share so many of her interests that she felt sure they would get along very well together. At first she did not question the fact that he had only given her his London address, yet wanted to meet her in Bournemouth. She asked him if he would telephone her, but he wrote back and said that he found talking on the telephone awkward, and

74

again suggested that she should write to him – at his London address – to arrange a meeting *in Bournemouth*.

Eventually Patricia began to suspect that everything was not as it should be. Peter was not in the London telephone book, but Patricia managed to obtain his number from an association of which he had told her he was a member. Her suspicions were confirmed when the phone was answered by Peter's long-suffering wife, and Patricia learnt that Peter was in the habit of meeting women through advertisements and having affairs with them. It seemed he was currently sleeping with a girlfriend in Bournemouth – but using his home address to make new contacts.

Said Patricia:

It was only a small thing – that he kept making excuses about phone calls – but it was enough to make me think twice about believing everything he said. It hasn't put me off the idea of advertising to meet people, as I'm sure that sort of thing is the exception rather than the rule.

9

What Really Matters

The case histories in Chapter 8 illustrate over and over again the importance of recognizing two elements of human behaviour that are most important in the making of close relationships: *trust* and *risk*.

To learn how much you can trust a stranger, and what degree of risk you are prepared to take in testing this trust out is something that you will only learn by your own experience of other people. But looking at other's successes and failures will make you more aware of what can, or might, happen for you in similar circumstances.

Learning from experience

Both Marion and Adrian were big losers, materially and emotionally, and while the circumstances of their cases differ, they had one thing in common. Both were blinded by their feelings and both trusted their partner far beyond the point that even they would have judged to be rational – had they not been so eager to please, in order to be accepted and loved.

They both said later that they would have behaved differently if they had visited the homes of Richard and Celia earlier in the affairs – that by doing this they would have learned more about them. They both felt that they had made an emotional commitment far too quickly – out of their need to 'have someone'. Both of them admitted later that if they had seen anyone else rush into the same situations with such speed, they would have thought them to be foolish, and yet when it came to themselves they lost their normal intelligent ability to stand outside the situation and make a sensible assessment. They not only ignored the warnings of friends who expressed concern about their new relationships, but cut themselves off from people whom they had known all their lives, as if to hide the relationships from them.

In taking responsibility for Richard's and Celia's financial difficulties both Marion and Adrian felt, *at the time*, that they were behaving in a generous and trusting way. That was the risk they took, and the trust they gave. But in neither case was it deserved.

Penny took a different kind of risk when she decided that having young children was something that she would advertise, not hide. Her risk paid off, because it attracted a man who thrived with a readymade family. It would have been a greater risk if she had tried to discount the importance of her children to her, for she may then have found herself having to make choices between them and a person who really was not interested in them.

Helen took a tremendous leap of faith when she packed her bags and went off to stay with Douglas. But she knew when she did so that she was not emotionally involved with him, or he with her, so that in one sense she took no risk at all – apart from the trust which she gave him when she went into his home. She had made a 'gut' judgement of his character – and he of hers.

Patricia also made a 'gut' judgement when she decided to ferret out Peter's telephone number. She wasn't quite sure what it was that left her not wanting to take the risk of believing all he said in his letters – apart from a vague nagging feeling that all was not as it should be. But Patricia is the kind of person who trusts her intuition – and in affairs of the heart often this is a better voice to listen to than the one that is busy trying to persuade you that you are about to go off hand in hand into the sunset, as Adrian believed.

It would have been easy for Dave to have ignored his reaction to Jennie's love of country and western music. Many would not feel so strongly about musical tastes as to want to discontinue a relationship that seemed so good in other areas. But he was right to do so, for he had already had a bad experience involving differing musical tastes. He used the experience to learn a little more about himself, and would be much more searching in his questions about musical tastes in first contacts in the future. Although cancelling that first date might have dented Jennie's feelings, it would have been less considerate to have gone along with it when Dave had such strong reservations.

Proceeding with caution

If you have reached the point of a first meeting, gone home from it with the hope that it will not be the last, and allowed yourself to sleep on it for at least one night, what should your next move be, assuming that you feel just as enthusiastic as you did the night before?

Marion, Adrian and Patricia would tell you to proceed *with caution*. Try to recognize what percentage of your enthusiasm is for the *real* person you have met, and what percentage is simply your relief that you may have 'found someone'. How much of your good feelings at this moment are due to the real qualities of your prospect, and how much are they due to your imagination drawing you pictures of a blissful domestic scene in a rosecovered cottage?

Try using a pen and paper to write down what you actually know about the other, and what you are simply hoping is true – perhaps with no basis at all. What are the gaps in your knowledge of the other person? What do you need to know before even considering an emotional commitment – assuming that the other person wants this too. Are there simple questions that you can ask at your next meeting, which perhaps you were afraid to ask at the first?

Are there any little whispers in the back of your mind which you would prefer to ignore, in case they spoil your fantasy of romance or security? Test this out by writing down any doubts that you have – often when they are brought up to a more conscious level, they will not seem as bad as you might have feared them to be.

What are your chances of visiting this person's home? Have they hinted that there are reasons why you should not? How would you feel about them visiting *your* home? Think about friends and relatives of yours with whom you have had good relationships for many years – how would they react to your newfound friend? This is not to suggest that it is up to them who you chose to become involved with, but your reactions to this mental test may cause or resolve anxieties about your judgement.

How much did your prospect tell you about past relationships? What was your reaction to it? Do you think that they had been unfairly treated? Were they fair to their past partner? Did they seem compelled to 'go on' about an ex-partner, to the exclusion of other topics?

Bear in mind that some people spend months, even years, searching for the right relationship. Finding it has just as much to do with it being the right time for the searcher, as it does with the character of the person sought. If you are seeking a serious relationship which you hope will end in marriage, avoid rushing any stage of your search.

Raymond met Angela as the result of replying to her advertisement. He lived in Central London, and as Angela was quite well off she did not need to work, and it became the habit for her to visit Raymond's home regularly. He became aware that she was more involved with him than he with her, and although he had hoped to find a permanent relationship, something about her held him back. Eventually it happened that he was travelling in the area where she lived, and he decided to surprise her with a visit. She lived in a very spacious house, and he was most impressed with the large and well-kept gardens. But when Angela opened the front door, he was appalled to find that the entire house was in a state of dirt and disrepair, with newspapers stacked in every available place, so there was scarcely room to move.

Angela did not seem to think that there was anything unusual about her home, but it was immediately clear to Raymond that he could not possibly live with a person who chose to live in such disorder. Neither was he the type of person who would risk hurting Angela's feelings by telling her of the effect her lifestyle had on his opinion of her. It had seemed quite reasonable that he had not visited her home for the six or seven months he had known her, but it would have saved a lot of heartbreak if he had managed to see much earlier what she found acceptable. All he had seen of her was as a visitor in *his* home – on her best behaviour, and with no responsibility for doing any of the usual domestic chores that it is safe to assume that most people are happy to perform.

Raymond says now that he has no regrets about the time he spent with Angela – she was good fun and they spent many hours enjoying each other's company. He knows that just having 'someone in his life' helped him through a period of great loneliness, and he is certain that the same was true for her. But he realizes how close he came to making a permanent commitment to her, and that could have been disastrous.

Remember each time you meet a new person through the medium of advertising that in just making the contact you are enriching yourself by the experience of allowing another's life to touch yours. Even a conversation on the telephone with someone you may never meet will add a new dimension – no matter how small – to your understanding of yourself and others. Try to take each step in the process of ending your loneliness slowly and carefully – in this way you will enjoy the journey as much as reaching your destination.

10

The Dangers,
and How to Avoid Them

I advertised for a wife-to-be [said Commander Darry-man, a 67-year old ex naval officer living in New Zealand] and one of those who replied, Mrs Veronica Tinne, a resident of Whitehawk with two teenage sons, seemed the most suitable. We had a strong mutual interest in sailing. Three months later, she and her sons arrived here and we were married on the quayside. When she asked if she might spend the night alone on my cruiser, the Spindrift, I agreed. But in the morning, she, her sons and the Spindrift had vanished and I have not seem them since.

(*Private Eye*, 'True Stories')

Many books will tell you how to 'improve' yourself, how to make yourself more attractive to the opposite sex. Many counsellors and other helping professionals are ready and willing to help you to 'look at yourself' and to make changes in your behaviour and thinking. They can be extremely helpful and supportive, but this book tries to help you to look at the *other person*, and to evaluate him or her. This chapter will help you to recognize the less desirable facets of the men or women you may meet as the result of your advertisement though, of course, you may see bits of yourself in some of the attitudes described.

Imagine for a moment that you are wandering alone and unarmed through a jungle. You know that there are many animals hidden amongst the trees. Some of them are friendly and harmless – but some are not. *You will not be able to discover which is which by looking in a mirror*. You will need to recognize the ones that are liable to hurt you, and the best way to do this is to know just what to look for, and to be able to approach them closely enough to see them clearly – but not so close that they will be able to bite you.

It may be that some of the following comments sound harsh, but the fact is that when you meet people through the medium of advertising, *you know nothing about them other than what they tell you*.

It is essential that you learn to listen very carefully to everything that is said and try to hear what thoughts and feelings lie behind the words. And remember, the kind of negative behaviour described here is a product of the times in which we live, and the people exhibiting it suffer as much, if not more, than the better adjusted people we may meet.

The timewasters

The most obvious danger for a man in the jungle of heart-search is the woman who is reasonably contented with her life – but bored. She wants the excitement of being wined, dined and desired, but is not prepared to make a long-term commitment to anybody. The reasons for this are many and varied, but whatever the cause she has often polished to a fine art the method of having one, two or even a dozen dates with any man who spends freely upon her, and who may fall for her before he realizes that she is not looking for a serious relationship.

Luckily, this woman is usually easy to recognize. She will often make the first telephone contact and it will be obvious that she is immediately available for a date. She will probably suggest meeting for a meal, but will not offer to pay her share. She will most likely be very charming company, but will avoid personal conversation. She may refer obliquely to her disappointment that other men friends do not 'treat her properly'; and she will give the impression of living a very full

82

social life. You may even begin to feel the need to compete with your 'rivals' by providing more and better meals and outings.

If in doubt, back out!

For the woman, the corresponding danger is not financial, but physical and emotional. The most frequent male predator who may be encountered is the one looking for yet another bed to clamber into. This type of man may make his intentions known fairly rapidly, and it is a sad reflection on the desperation of so many women for physical and emotional closeness, that he will score again and again. Since the so-called 'sexual revolution' casual sex has become the norm for so many, that a woman who wants to give warmth and care to a potential partner can easily be made to feel as though she is frigid or lacks the ability to 'give' if she is wary of falling into bed early in the relationship. In the long run, men are the losers when they demand immediate sexual involvement, for the woman who values herself is the only one who can offer real commitment. And there is also the danger, even with someone whose background you know, and far more with someone you know nothing about, of contracting serious, even fatal, sexually transmitted diseases.

If in doubt, back out!

Not so frequently encountered, but dangerous when they appear, are the moneyseekers. These are people of both sexes who are in real financial trouble: the woman who is having difficulties with her mortgage, the man whose business has failed, the helplessly and hopelessly unemployed, whose last resort is to try to find someone better off than they are who will rescue them. They may talk of nothing other than their shortage of money. They may not divulge the degree of their insolvency until they are sure that their victim is beginning to feel attached to them. They may spend what little money they

83

have quite freely to impress the other party, dropping only occasional hints about the price of things; some will go to quite elaborate lengths to invent a sudden hard-luck story. This may be prefaced by something like 'I've fallen in love with you, but I can't pretend – I've just lost my job, crashed my car, lost my house to my ex-wife or husband', etc., etc.

Many are the heartsearchers who have allowed such people to actually move into their homes before realizing that all they have found is a financial liability – a person who has not, for whatever reason, been able to make it without battening on to a more complete and successful person.

If in doubt, back out!

The heartbreakers

Nothing ever goes right for me, but now that I've met you, it will all be different.

This of course, may turn out to be true. Often two people who care for each other produce a partnership in which they can pool their various talents and material wealth to make a better world for both. But beware the partner who has an almost magical belief in it 'just happening'. It may be that they have failed dismally with everything they have tried: marriage, career, all the things that go to make up a contented life. No wonder – if they really believe that they cannot make it alone. These people are likely to be bowled over by the success you have made of your life, and want to have a piece of the action. And if they really believe in magic, then they will not be able to get past the first setbacks. They will believe that it was 'not meant to be' and give up. You will be left to carry the burden of the breaking relationship. They will add yet another failure to the list of the things that 'never go right', with which they regaled you so enthusiastically a few weeks or months earlier.

If in doubt, back out!

I need someone to look after me.

All of us have some remnants of our parents lurking within us, and there is no harm in that. It is the part of us which makes us able to put aside our own needs to help a person who is in some kind of difficulty – perhaps sick, or in need of a helping hand over a rough patch. It can respond very strongly to a plea for help, and if it did not, we would be lacking in the basics of compassion for our fellows. But if the need to be 'looked after' does not ring warning bells for you, look again at what the words are saying. What kind of adult person needs to be 'looked after'? And who was 'looking after' them before you came along, in answer, perhaps to an advertised plea? Was it a parent, spouse, a previous man-friend or woman-friend? What became of them? Did they tire when they found that the more 'looking after' they did, the more was demanded of them? *Listen carefully to everything they say.* Are they perhaps the sort of inadequate person who will expect you to 'look after' them like a small child? Make their decisions for them? Take responsibility for the pace of the relationship? Do they seem to lack opinions on most subjects? Do they tell you of all the problems they had when they were left to cope on their own? How much of a parent do you want to be? Do you really want to be strong enough for two, or are you seeking a relationship in which *everything* is shared?

If in doubt, back out!

All the women in my life have been bitches, but you're different.

or

All the men in my life have been swine, but you're different.

What person will not be flattered by this comment, and determined to strive even harder to prove that they are,

85

indeed, able to succeed where their predecessors have failed! But look for a moment at what these words really mean. Everyone has the opportunity throughout their lives to meet a wide variety of people.

There *are* 'bitches and swine' but the great majority of people are neither. Those who see their lives and relationships in these terms are, first and foremost, very bitter. To make any kind of concession to others' imperfections will be almost impossible for them, for part of their game is blame. It is likely that they will also talk of the number of times that they have been rejected. Be sure that their past loves would be very surprised to hear that, for they would have felt, by the insistence that they should be 'different', that *they* were the rejected ones.

For whatever reason, these people have been unable (*because of their methods of choosing, or because they are never satisfied*) to form satisfactory relationships. Again, the counsellors would be ready to tell us why this is, and perhaps to help us to 'understand'. But listen carefully; underneath the bitterness there is something else. The 'other person' is always at fault and when the first flush of love has subsided, chances are you will be blamed for the things which will inevitably go wrong, for every new partnership needs to have the rough edges ground off, and that means making concessions on both sides.

The best that can be hoped for in a relationship with this person is that you do indeed manage to offer the honesty that past 'failed' partners did not give. Remembering that most humans do have the potential to grow, it may well be worth the effort. But be careful, for you could simply become the next recipient of their bitterness and criticism.

Only you can make the decision on how far you are prepared to go in another's interests, and we have all heard dreadful stories of those who have found themselves almost destroyed by the effort. The tragedy of the embittered is that they so often lose what is freely offered to them because the experiences *which they have chosen, over and over again* compound their belief that to be close is to be hurt. While they leave a trail of bewildered and broken hearts behind them, they are storing up for themselves great loneliness, for they will eventually run out of opportunities.

If in doubt, back out!

Think again

Perhaps in reading the above you will have spotted an experience which you have already had. Try to remember what it meant to you at the time, and how it ended. Ask yourself if you would recognize it if it happened again, and how you would react. Perhaps it is attractive, even to you, to have another person very dependent upon you; perhaps even you get a secret sense of pleasure from rejection – proving yet again that there is something wrong with you – or 'them'.

If, as you were reading, you told yourself that you wouldn't mind *any* of the situations described, then maybe you are still at the point that many advertisers are. Perhaps you are thinking *anyone* is better than no-one. *Think again*; this is the kind of desperation which can lead you into a completely unsuitable and possibly painful situation. Remember that beginning a new relationship is not like buying a new washing machine. You cannot return your partner to the shop if things go wrong. Of course, you can walk out on a relationship at any time, but once your feelings are engaged this will never be easy, no matter how tough the going gets. It is the ability and need of human beings to become involved *emotionally* with others that provides the two great opposites of human experience: the joy, love and closeness of a caring relationship (the very cornerstone of our social structure); and the grief and pain which come with the loss of our dreams. Without one, we could not have the other.

Be aware that many people in search of 'someone new' may be in fact trying to find a salve for a relationship which is breaking, but has not broken. Again beware. It is most difficult for many people to have a period of no involvement; they do not want to let go of the old until they have found the new. In some circumstances this may not be a bad thing, and certainly many divorced parents who still have contact over children may continue their relationship for years, though they may see it as no more than is necessary.

The experiences of many suggest that a three-to-four month break from a previous relationship – that is, a voluntary choice not to get in touch, no matter how much one wants to – would demonstrate the end of a deep involvement. But we all know and understand the dangers of the 'rebound' affair, or marriage.

Think about your own last relationship. Is it really over? How long is it since you have seen your ex-partner? Do you still harbour dreams that one day a miracle will occur and it will turn out right after all? How do you feel about being 'on your own' for a while? Do you need more time to recover, no matter how difficult it seems, before you become involved again?

I said at the beginning of this chapter that looking in a mirror would not tell us which of the animals to avoid in the jungle. But it is to be hoped that the look we have taken at some of them has taught us something about ourselves.

11

Ordinary People

We live in an age which encourages us to believe in the impossible. Every day we see advertisements in magazines and newspapers telling us how we can change our lives for the better by eating a new chocolate bar or smoking another packet of cigarettes. The images the advertisers link with consumer goods are more often than not connected with the glamour of a man–woman relationship.

Our homes reflect the sort of lifestyle our grandparents could only have dreamed about. The scrubbed wooden table and paperlined shelves have been replaced by marbled formica and kitchen units. The electric kettle – once a luxury – can be seen in nearly every home, and menus that used to be the reserve of the wealthy can now be served without doing much more than defrosting a packet and popping it into the microwave.

We are inundated with images of beautiful women attracting handsome men, wealthy men attracting smart and successful career women. Money, large cars, boats, expensive perfumes, exclusive restaurants and glamorous sporting activities are displayed for us on television in ever-increasing volume. Television advertisements are often now presented as mini-dramas, telling a romantic or exciting story, always with a happy ending as the ice-cream is eaten, the cigar smoked, the lady won or the man ensnared.

In series after series, soap opera after soap opera, we gaze entranced as perfect marriage after perfect marriage is made, problem upon problem is solved. With the exception of a few programmes life is represented on the grand scale, and we all know as we turn off the television set that life for us is more ordinary, a bit more of a struggle, and we are unlikely to reach a stage in our existence when troubles fade away and all we have to look forward to are pleasure and contentment.

But do we really accept that? How often do the lonely dream about how good life will be when they meet their ideal match? How *then* they will be able to have the skiing holiday they always dreamed of? The house they always wanted? The romantic moments under the stars? The hours on a sun-drenched beach?

How much do the lonely assume it is their aloneness which makes them unable to live life to the full? How often have you said about an outing, an activity, a holiday, 'If only I had someone to go with'? How often have you made the decision to remain isolated or unhappy, because you feel life is being unfair to you? And how much does it really matter if you do – as long as you believe that out there somewhere is the person who will transform your life?

I believe it does matter, for it seems to me that in order to have a good relationship with someone else, two things are necessary. First, you must have a good relationship with yourself; and second, you must be able to tell the difference between reality and fantasy.

It is impossible in the context of this book to tell you *how* to have a good relationship with yourself, but I can tell you what life is like for people who have the gift of enjoying their own company. They will not be disabled by loneliness, though if they have been through the pain of losing a partner they may have spent some time, long or short, holding others at bay. This is a normal process of self-healing, but it will not blight their life, and as they begin to feel whole again, they will venture back into the world, with or *without* a partner.

They will not be afraid to go out on their own, whether for a walk in the country, or to the cinema or even to a restaurant, perhaps with a book or newspaper tucked under their arm. They will accept the invitations of friends of the same sex to spend time with them, without feeling like a burden. They will be prepared to take the risk of going on holiday by themselves, knowing that if they are open to new friendships there will be plenty of opportunities to begin them.

They will not deprive themselves of new clothes 'because they have no-one to wear them for'. They will use their own knowledge of loneliness to allow them to recognize and respond to the same signs in others.

They will cook themselves proper meals, because they know that their health is as important during their period of aloneness as it is when they have someone with whom to share a meal. They will be able to enjoy going to a class or club, and to continue to enjoy it even when they have seen that their Prince or Princess Charming is not likely to be among their classmates.

In other words they will not give up on life and wait to be rescued by a mysterious stranger who may not even exist. And that brings us to the second necessity – that of knowing the difference between reality and fantasy.

If you glance through the columns of heartsearch advertisements you will come across advertisements which at first glance seem attractive: 'Millionaire with own yacht'; 'Lovely blonde. Successful model', and so on. Remember our American friend who wanted her Edward Fox lookalike? These advertisements are the extreme end of the spectrum, and it is tempting to ask why a rich man with a yacht or a beautiful model do not have full social lives and find it quite unnecessary to advertise for company.

But is it as easy as that to dismiss the fantasies conjured up by such advertisements? No matter how hard we try to keep a balanced view of the world, modern life with the help of television has made it easy for most of us to believe in the impossible dream. It is so much more pleasant to believe that life *can* be lived on a sun-drenched beach; that the day-to-day problems of life *will* magically disappear; that knights in shining white armour, and beautiful damsels who do nothing but smile lovingly at their men, are in great supply.

Don't let fantasy allow you to throw away what may not be the crock at the end of the rainbow, but could, with a little effort and commonsense and caring – about yourself, too – be nurtured into a lasting and trusting relationship.

The world in which we live is an ordinary world in many respects, and it is populated by ordinary people; people who must work for their living; who only go on one holiday a year, and not always to Greece or the Costa del Sol; people who will flower when they feel valued, though they may not have won the football pools. Ordinariness is not something to be scorned, for it is what most of us have in common.

And love? Where does love fit into this world of advertisements and letters and telephone calls? Is love something that just 'happens' when two people meet and get on well? Or is it something that has to be worked at, something that can give great pain as well as great contentment? What a pity there are no simple answers to these questions! How many times have you seen two people struggling on in a marriage which appears to you to be painful and unsuccessful and wondered why on earth they did not call an end to it all – give up, and look for someone new.

Perhaps there are some who believe that all they deserve is what they have, no matter how unsatisfactory. That no matter what they do, they will not find happiness, so they may as well stay where they are rather than make the effort to move on to yet another painful situation. Certain types of Christianity have put a tremendous burden of guilt on people, and the idea of 'hell of earth' in exchange for 'heaven later' is accepted by so many.

But in the making of a new relationship it is worth remembering that no human being is perfect, and we cannot expect perfection, either in ourselves or our partners. We must be prepared, unless we are lucky enough to have met our mirror images – and how boring that might be – to balance our giving and taking. Giving till it hurts will not help anyone.

Losing our own life in another person's can only result in the loss of our own self-esteem. In our commitment to the relationship, we must not lose sight of our commitment to our self.

If you love someone then you will value their wellbeing as much as you value your own. Not more. Not less. *The same*. You cannot love another 'successfully' unless you love yourself.

Good luck with your search!

Overcoming Common Problems

A successful and popular series to give you practical
help for the emotional and medical problems of
everyday life.

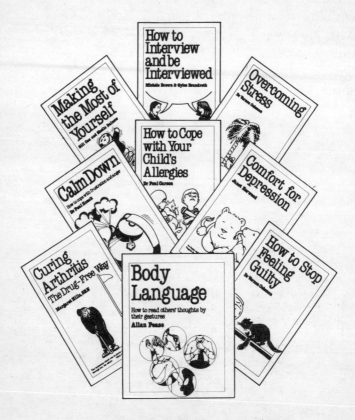

Paperbacks £1·95 to £4·95
Available from all good bookshops

 For a complete list of titles write to;
Sheldon Press Mail Order,
SPCK, Marylebone Road, London NW1 4DU

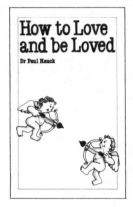